Before You Turn the Page

The book you hold in your hand is the birth of an idea whose time has come.

For many years George Vandeman has dreamed of demonstrating by voice and pen the fulfillment of one of the Bible's choicest predictions—a prediction found in the heart of the treasured Old Testament classic, Isaiah. Its author has often been called the gospel prophet because he was foremost in foretelling the coming of the Saviour, the Lord Jesus Christ.

In fact, in his famed fifty-eighth chapter is Scripture's finest statement of true religion. This chapter does not simply teach God's message, but does so with urgency and conviction, giving down-to-earth instruction to "free the heavy burdens," "let the oppressed go free," "deal your bread to the hungry," and "clothe the unclothed." As a result of following this counsel, joy, peace, and prosperity will break forth as can scarcely be imagined.

But then, these verses predict a final last-day restoration. "Those from among you shall build the old waste places; you shall raise up the foundations of many generations; and you shall be called the Repairer of the Breach, the Restorer of Streets to Dwell In." Isaiah 58:12.

Could this clear statement of God's plan include a restoration of truth lost and confused through the centuries?

Does this prediction complement the message of Scripture's last book of Revelation, which describes the recovery of neglected truth as an essential part of last-day events?

The answer to these questions—which follows in these pages—should be for you the unfolding of a thrilling drama, a drama in which you may participate not simply as a passive bystander but by becoming totally and happily involved.

You will discover how easy it is to build encouraging bridges of understanding between the denominations—bridges that can help us discover God's plan for our lives.

The idea given birth in this book is simply to detail how God used the reformers—the founders of the various churches—in recovering neglected truth and restoring that neglected truth to its rightful place in the Christian church. It will give the reader an inspiring overview of the reformation still active in our day. We hope you will find this book explaining, as no other book has done quite so clearly, why there are so many denominations and churches.

Please note that the book is also the by-product of an unusual series of television programs in the "It Is Written" tradition. Pastor Vandeman has invited the leaders of these churches to meet with him personally as their church is being featured.

All this and more will be found in the pages that follow.

The Publishers.

In Appreciation

My wife Nellie has known of my long-time dream of seeing the television series and this book by the same name ready for the public. Her encouragement has helped to keep that dream alive and progressing.

The magnitude of the project, however, at times hindered its progress. Extreme care and exhaustive research were needed to treat each denomination or church with impeccable fairness and accuracy. The overseas mission of television shooting to reconstruct the founders' early roots was in itself a major project. These factors, along with the huge amount of funds needed to bring these programs to the masses, resulted in delay after delay.

But now, providentially, I believe, the pieces of the fascinating puzzle are falling into place.

I want to thank my faithful secretary, Frances Williams, and the "It Is Written" office family for their part in living with the pressure of this time of serious preparation. Martin Weber, my assistant in research and writing, has worked tirelessly to help bring together the story about to unfold in these pages.

And to the Holy Spirit, we all acknowledge our dependence for producing this work which could profoundly affect so many lives.

We hope you like the television series and the book—and that you will join with us in ascribing glory to our Lord and Saviour, Jesus Christ, for He alone is worthy.

George Vandeman

Contents

What I Like About the Lutherans   9
What I Like About the Baptists   21
What I Like About the Methodists   33
What I Like About the Charismatics   47
What I Like About the Catholics   61
What I Like About Our Jewish Friends   73
Why So Many Denominations?   85
What I Like About the Adventists   97

Dr. Oswald C. J. Hoffman, for thirty years the speaker of the popular "Lutheran Hour" radio program, speaks with George Vandeman in St. Louis, Missouri. St. Louis is the home of the Lutheran Laymen's League, the sponsoring organization for this international broadcast.

What I Like About the Lutherans 1521

Come with me to the beautiful valley of the Rhine River. The peaceful setting belies the unrest that rippled through Europe in the early sixteenth century.

Picture the scene that fateful spring afternoon of April 18, 1521. There stands a young German priest, defending himself against charges of heresy. Surrounding him are princes, proud nobles, honored generals, and church leaders. Everyone in that historic hall bends forward to catch each syllable from the lips of the lonely crusader.

"I cannot and I will not retract. It is unsafe for a Christian to speak against his conscience. Here I stand. I cannot do otherwise. May God help me! Amen."

With these ringing words Martin Luther launched the Protestant Reformation. His bold stand marked a turning point in history.

Was Luther able to complete the Reformation? Or is that left for us today?

Back in sixteenth-century Germany, the future of Christianity hung in the balance. Luther, a university professor, had challenged the church's claim of the right to control personal faith. His teachings aroused religious and political turmoil throughout the vast territory known as the Holy Roman Empire. Something had to be done to quell the crisis. Finally Emperor Charles V summoned

Luther to appear before a general council at Worms.

While Luther's exact words at his trial are uncertain today, there is no doubt about his message. Conscience must
answer to God alone. Salvation comes freely by faith
alone. The Bible is the source of spiritual authority, not
church tradition or the decrees of its leaders.

This was truth that had been lost for centuries. The
time had come to bring it back.

Luther stood alone at Worms. The emperor scoffed,
"This monk will never make a heretic out of me!" As expected, the council condemned Luther. He was forbidden
to teach and was stripped of his civil rights. His books
were burned—but the message they carried survived the
smoke and the flames.

Despite widespread scorn and persecution, Luther's
message took hold in the hearts of the common people.
And eight years after the council at Worms, a group of
German princes took their stand with Luther. They
formed an alliance protesting the church's attempt to
crush the Reformation. From this protest of the princes at
Spires in 1529, the term *Protestant* was born.

Luther's teachings spread to all of Europe, especially
Scandinavia. Followers of Luther crossed the Atlantic
early in colonial history. At Hudson's Bay in 1619, they
celebrated their first Christmas in America.

Early churches organized by poor Lutheran immigrants
were small, often lacking pastors. But as Lutheran settlers continued to flock to the United States, the denomination grew rapidly. Congregations became linked together in groups known as synods.

American Lutherans today are spread among a dozen
separate synods. Just a few of the synods account for the
great majority of our more than 8 million Lutherans. And
further merging is in process. The Lutheran Church in
America—the largest group—and the American Lutheran

Church—third largest—are uniting. The Association of Evangelical Lutheran Churches is joining hands with them. This new synod will have more than 5 million baptized members.

The second-largest Lutheran organization, with 2.7 million members, is the Missouri Synod. From their headquarters in St. Louis, they operate the world's oldest religious radio station. "The Lutheran Hour," supported by the Lutheran Laymen's League, is heard in more than 100 countries. Dr. Oswald Hoffman, my cherished friend, has been the beloved speaker of that broadcast for more than thirty years. I thank God for preserving his forceful and fruitful ministry. We talked together in St. Louis:

VANDEMAN: Dr. Oswald Hoffman of "The Lutheran Hour"—I'm delighted to have you with me today.

HOFFMAN: Thank you, Dr. Vandeman. It's my privilege to be here. We Lutherans have a great respect for you and your people, who began broadcasting on radio so very early—and then on television at the very beginning when it was coming into its own. And you've used it for the proclamation of the gospel throughout the world.

VANDEMAN: Thank you kindly. For years you have been a real inspiration to me. You've enriched my ministry. So I think I know what you're going to say when I ask you, Why are you personally a Lutheran Christian?

HOFFMAN: Well, I'm a Christian because I'm a follower of Jesus Christ. I'm a Lutheran, not because I follow Martin Luther, but because, like Luther, I owe my allegiance to Jesus Christ. Luther came through a terrific experience in order to make this great discovery. He was led by soul struggle to find that the gospel does not depend

upon the works that we contribute, but that it is depen-
dent upon the goodness and grace of God that comes out of
His heart to human beings and is shown to the world in
Jesus Christ. That's the gospel.

VANDEMAN: And it thrills us through and through to
hear how you tell it. You say Martin Luther made a great
discovery. Was this "neglected truth" then, in a sense?

HOFFMAN: It was—it certainly was. It was not that it
was absent before. It had been a part of the tradition of the
church since the apostolic age, but the rubbish of the ages
had gathered around it, and people came to think of themselves as making a great contribution to all this. But Luther said No. After studying the Scriptures, he learned
that the contribution to our salvation comes from God. It
is from God that you are in Christ Jesus—as St. Paul said
to the Corinthians. The man who is made just by faith will
live. And Luther became the man that he was—a robust
character filled with faith and with love, by which faith
expresses itself. Martin Luther was a man who was at his
best when he talked about faith and also about love.

VANDEMAN: And he translated the Bible into the language of the common people.

HOFFMAN: He certainly did—and it was a beautiful
translation. For Luther, behind every word of the Greek
and Hebrew text of the Scriptures stood the majesty of
God. But he translated the Bible into the language people
were speaking at that time. He put the Scriptures into
language every peasant could understand, and the gospel
came through. By the power of the Spirit it took hold of the
hearts of people and brought them to faith in Christ.

VANDEMAN: Thank you. You've been so gracious. I wish I had an hour to talk to you about this great truth. But suppose Martin Luther should be resurrected today and mingle among us again. Would he feel comfortable in the church that bears his name?

HOFFMAN: Well, 450 years have gone by since that time, and you can't ignore history. Some problems have been solved. Other problems have arisen. But I have a feeling, just a personal feeling, that if Luther came on the scene and looked at the church that calls itself Lutheran, he would have something to say to all of us. And one of the things he would say is, "You've got to get with the gospel. Without the gospel, you are nothing at all. You must proclaim the gospel with all the authority of God. You must bring the good news of forgiveness that people actually possess by the grace of God through faith in Jesus Christ."

VANDEMAN: I agree. Thank you so much, Dr. Hoffman. We all appreciate what you have said.

Yes, untold millions join Lutherans in cherishing the heritage of Martin Luther. I count myself among them. There is so much I like about the Lutheran Church. I admire them for putting their faith to work in society. They provide orphanages, hospitals, treatment centers for alcoholics, and homes for the elderly.

Let me say it again—there are so many things I like about my Lutheran friends. But there's one thing I especially appreciate, as I mentioned a moment ago: The Lutheran movement was called by God to champion a neglected truth—the glorious teaching of salvation by faith alone. Luther cleared away the cobwebs of the Dark Ages and restored the foundation of the gospel.

Luther's journey toward truth is a fascinating story.

The summer after his college graduation he had a horrifying encounter with death. While walking home from visiting his parents, a violent thunderstorm burst upon him. Lightning hurled him to the ground. Cowering in terror, he cried, "St. Anne, help me! I will become a monk."

He kept his promise. Luther entered the monastery at Erfurt and was ordained in 1507. Contemplating his first celebration of mass, he felt overwhelmed by unworthiness. How could a sinner stand in God's holy presence unless he himself were holy?

So Luther determined to become holy. He pursued purity by depriving himself of life's comforts—even its necessities. Some nights, shivering under slim covers, he would console himself, "I have done nothing wrong today." Then misgivings would arise. "Have I fasted enough? Am I poor enough? Am I pure enough?"

Nothing he could do brought him peace. He could never be certain he had satisfied God. But finally he discovered that the peace he was trying so hard to obtain was available as a gift. The truth which set him free came to him in the New Testament book of Romans. He learned that God Himself was punished as sinners deserve, so we could be forgiven—freely forgiven—in the Lord Jesus Christ.

Luther could hardly believe this good news. Despite his guiltiness he could be credited with holiness—because Jesus, who really was holy, suffered his penalty.

Of course, the church had always pointed sinners to come to God for salvation. But Luther introduced a vital new dimension. He discovered that believers, even though sinful, can at the same time be counted righteous. You see, God considers sinners to be saints as soon as they trust in Jesus—even before their lives reveal good works (which, of course, will be forthcoming). Romans 4:5 says so: "To him who does not work but believes on Him who justifies the ungodly, his faith is accounted for righteousness."

So the ungodly who surrender to Jesus, you see, are justified. Forgiveness comes not because we are holy. Not by works, Luther now realized, but because we trust in Jesus.

All his life Luther had thought it would be unjust to reward sinners with eternal life. So he believed in purgatory, where imperfections were said to be purged away after death to make Christians fit for heaven. He sincerely thought that in purgatory the faithful will be cleansed of sin so God can claim them as His own.

Luther also believed that suffering in purgatory could be shortened by receiving an indulgence from the church. These indulgences were granted to those who visited shrines of the saints and viewed their relics.

Luther had thought these saints had stored up extra measures of Christ's goodness which they could share with sinners. But now he learned that "all have sinned and fall short of the glory of God." Romans 3:23. Paul himself said that everyone falls short. Even the saints must put their hope in the Lord Jesus Christ.

And because Christ is our substitute, every Christian is already worthy of heaven. On the cross, God "qualified us to be partakers of the inheritance of the saints." Colossians 1:12. No need for purgatory!

Joy filled Luther's heart. Finally his troubled conscience found peace. But the gospel that soothed his own soul sparked conflict with the church.

The battle broke out over indulgences. Wittenberg's castle church featured a collection of famous relics. Among them was a thorn certified to have pierced Christ's brow at Calvary. The relics went on display every All Saints Day. Pilgrims came from near and far to Wittenberg seeking indulgences.

Luther yearned to share the good news that had set him free. On October 31, 1517, the eve of All Saints Day, he posted a list of ninety-five objections to the sale of indulgences. They were written in Luther's vintage style—crisp, bold, and unqualified.

The reformer challenged anyone to debate him. "Saints have no extra credits," he thundered. "And Christ's merits are freely available. If the pope does have power to release anyone from purgatory, why in the name of love does he not abolish purgatory by letting everyone out?"

Copies of Luther's theses spread throughout Europe, unleashing a storm. Luther had not intended to revolt, only to reform. But he was pronounced a rebel and a heretic. Luther was warned to recant, or the church would reluctantly punish him.

But the Reformer felt compelled to press on. He confided to a friend, "God does not guide me—He pushes me forward; He carries me away. I am not master of myself. I desire to live in repose, but I am thrown into the midst of tumults and revolutions."

Luther charged that the church interfered with a Christian's personal relationship with God. He proclaimed Jesus to be the only mediator between God and sinners. And "the true Christian pilgrimage is not to Rome, but to the prophets, the Psalms and the Gospels."

In so many ways, Luther, despite his love for the church, found himself splitting away from it. The separation became final when he condemned the church as antichrist.

Pope Leo X responded by excommunicating Luther on January 3, 1521. His writings were banned and burned. To all appearances, Luther himself would soon be put to the flames.

But Frederick, the elector of Saxony, determined to protect the Reformer. He prevailed upon Emperor Charles to provide a fair hearing for Luther in Germany. Charles finally agreed to provide such a hearing at Worms.

When Luther refused to recant, his friends hid him for safety in the Wartburg castle. During his exile, Luther translated the New Testament into German. Later he translated the Old Testament.

After ten months at Wartburg, Luther returned to Wittenberg and resumed leadership of the Reformation. Problems abounded. Fanatics had abused popular religious zeal. And in 1525 came the Peasants' War—a revolt against the princes. Luther received severe censure for refusing to support the peasants' political demands.

Conflict followed Luther throughout his life. Sometimes the Reformer erred in judgment. What else could we expect, since he had led the way out of such darkness?

So it was that Luther began the Reformation. He never claimed to have finished the restoration of truth. He said the work must continue even after he passed on.

Luther did die before his dreams were fulfilled. You see, problems in the church had developed over the centuries, and it would take centuries of reform to solve them. And the fight of faith isn't finished yet, even today.

Have you ever wondered how the church had fallen into the Dark Ages? There were many factors, of course, but let me give you some background. In the early days of Christianity, after the apostles died, some unfortunate events took place. The church drifted from its pure faith and fell away from Bible truth.

This was sad, but only to be expected—the apostle Paul had predicted it. He said that after his death, heresy would waylay the church. This took place just as the Scriptures foretold. It didn't happen overnight. The decay of truth spanned centuries.

At first the enemies of Christ had tried to destroy the church with persecution. Nero and other Roman emperors ravaged the first-century Christians. But amazingly, the gospel prospered under outright attack. The fires of persecution purified the church and sparked the spread of truth. The blood of the martyrs was as seed that sprang up everywhere.

Having failed at persecuting the church, the enemy changed his tactics. He determined to undermine Christianity from within. Using clever compromises and false teachings, he succeeded in crippling the faith once delivered to the saints. For centuries, the truth lay buried beneath tradition. Rites and ceremonies and teachings that Paul or Peter never heard of crept into the church.

But Heaven was not caught unprepared. In one sweeping movement which we call the Reformation, God reversed the trend of apostasy. Light began to break through. Reformers like Martin Luther restored truth which had so long been held from the people.

One fellow Reformer of Luther's was John Calvin. For many years Calvin labored with astounding success in Geneva, Switzerland. Along with his ability to communicate the gospel, Calvin was a brilliant scholar. Christians everywhere have been blessed by his writings.

Today various Reformed churches and the Presbyterians trace their roots to John Calvin. I wish we had an extra chapter in this book to talk with Presbyterians. Some of my closest friends in the Lord are of the Presbyterian faith. I rejoice with them in the good news of the gospel championed by Calvin and Luther.

But we know that the Reformation didn't end hundreds of years ago when the Reformers died. It had only just begun. Others continued their good work. In this book we will see how God used the Baptists, the Methodists—and other groups as well—to carry forward the torch of the Reformation.

Since all these churches brought back forgotten truth, could it be that there is more? More neglected truth to discover today? Something to think about, isn't it?

Whatever truths we may rediscover in God's Word, we will never cease to stand on Luther's shoulders. The gospel he proclaimed still beats in the heart of every Christian.

Without question, Luther remains one of the most re-markable Christians who ever lived. Fearless leader, in-spiring preacher, prolific writer, tender father—few have matched his contributions. Few have changed the course of history as he has.

More than anything else, Luther was a man of God. When burdened and oppressed, he fled for refuge to the Almighty's everlasting arms. During one particularly dark hour when the Reformation seemed doomed, he para-phrased the forty-sixth psalm in song. Protestants and Catholics alike treasure that hymn today—"A Mighty Fortress Is Our God." Notice the faith-inspiring words of the third verse—a verse we often overlook:

> And though this world, with devils filled,
> Should threaten to undo us,
> We will not fear, for God hath willed
> His truth to triumph through us.
>
> The prince of darkness grim,
> We tremble not for him;
> His rage we can endure,
> For lo! his doom is sure,
> One little word shall fell him.

Think of it! One little word from our Lord Jesus Christ, and Satan's host must flee.

Friend, are you oppressed by the enemy right now? One word from Heaven can rescue you. Are you burdened by guilt or fear? Perhaps by loneliness or a sense of failure? Maybe sickness or sorrow?

Let me assure you of this. The same God who guided and provided for Martin Luther loves you just as much today. He wants to be your mighty fortress too. Come without delay for the help and healing you desire.

Dr. James Draper, recent past president of the Southern Baptist Convention. Southern Baptist Convention presidents are chosen for a single-year term with a double term as a limit. Dr. James Draper preceded Dr. Charles Stanley of Atlanta, Georgia.

What I Like About the Baptists 1636

It happened amid the bitter cold of January 1636. An exiled preacher fled from home and plunged into the Massachusetts forest. Fourteen weeks he wandered in the snow, barely surviving. By day he hunted whatever food the birds failed to find. By night he shivered inside the shelter of a hollow log.

At last he found refuge with the Indians. Buying land from them, Roger Williams founded the colony of Providence in what is now Rhode Island. It became the capital of freedom in the New World—and the home of the first Baptist church in America.

Roger Williams's new colony should not have been necessary. After all, it was for freedom's sake that the Puritans had come to Massachusetts. They crossed the Atlantic, escaping persecution by the state church of England—only to create a state church of their own. All citizens were required to support the clergy. Magistrates waged war on heresy. Freedom of conscience suffocated in this Old-World-style connection of religion and government.

When Roger Williams first arrived in the Massachusetts Bay Colony, he found a warm welcome. The authorities even invited him to lead Boston's only church. But Williams declined. He could not support the suppression of conscience by government. He knew that most of history's bloody battles have been fought to enforce faith. And all for nothing. True Christianity, you see, cannot be compelled or legislated.

"Magistrates may decide what is due from man to man," Williams said. "But when they attempt to prescribe a man's duties to God, they are out of place." Williams also taught that no one should be forced to support the clergy.

"What?" exclaimed the authorities. "Is not the laborer worthy of his hire?" "Yes," Williams replied, "from them that hire him."

Puritan leaders could not tolerate such "new and dangerous opinions." At a formal trial, they condemned Williams and ordered him exiled. So, banned in Boston, he established in Providence the first modern government offering full freedom of conscience. Providence became the blueprint of the American Constitution a century and a half later.

Williams invited all the persecuted and oppressed to find refuge in Providence, whatever their faith. Even if they had no faith, they were welcome. Amid such a setting of freedom, the Baptist church found roots in America.

Baptists have always flourished in this land of liberty—their democratic and informal worship suits our national style. They have become the largest Protestant denomination in the United States.

Our nearly thirty million Baptists are spread among 100,000 local churches. These churches belong to various groups known as conventions. The largest by far is the Southern Baptist Convention, with half of the Baptists in America as members.

Even though local churches may be linked in a convention, each congregation retains independent government. This makes it all the more remarkable that Baptists are so involved in world evangelism.

Baptists differ widely in their beliefs. Some are conservative; others rather liberal. Some Baptists closely follow the teachings of John Calvin, the Reformer. Others do not.

Yet whatever their differences, Baptists are united in respect for the Scriptures as the only source of truth. Most other Protestants and Catholics have their creeds, but Baptists acknowledge no standard but the Bible—as they understand it, of course.

Baptists also agree that no human has the right to choose religion for another—not even parents for their children. So Baptists don't baptize babies. Instead, they dedicate their newborns to God, just as Mary and Joseph dedicated Baby Jesus. Then as Baptist children grow older, they are free to choose for themselves whether or not to be baptized.

Baptists have a history of bringing religious freedom from their homes into society. Like their forefather Roger Williams, many Baptists still believe in protecting the separation between church and state.

We all know that Baptists have a genius for producing great preachers. Among the most famous was Charles Spurgeon. Today we have Charles Stanley, W. A. Criswell, and, of course, our beloved Billy Graham.

Another Baptist, Dr. James Draper, is past president of the vast Southern Baptist Convention. We spoke together in Dallas, Texas.

VANDEMAN: Dr. Draper, I wish you could know how pleased I am to have you with me today.

DRAPER: Thank you so much, George. I'm delighted to be here.

VANDEMAN: Jimmy (that's what you asked me to call you), why are you personally a Baptist Christian?

DRAPER: Well, the first reason would be that my parents were very active Baptists. My dad was a preacher, and my granddad was a preacher.

VANDEMAN: You're a P.K., then—a preacher's kid?

DRAPER: That's right. So all my life I have been taught the Word of God. I grew up in a family that loved the Lord. My mother and dad led me to Christ. As I came to an age of understanding that I was a sinner and needed to be saved, I committed my life to Christ and was baptized and joined the Baptist Church. And then over the years the Baptist Church and Baptist institutions have nurtured me and encouraged me, trained me, educated me, so I guess the first reason I'm a Baptist would be that these are my roots. This is the atmosphere in which I found the Lord.

VANDEMAN: A blessed heritage, I would say. Aren't those early years the most impressionable?

DRAPER: There's no doubt about it. In fact, Christianity at its strongest is family Christianity, where the families are committed to the Lord. So we have a great heritage here.

Then I'm a Baptist Christian because I'm convicted of the great teachings and the great heritage of the Baptist people. Baptists have always emphasized the authority of the Word of God. We also believe in the autonomy of the local church—each congregation is self-governing. And the priesthood of the believer—every individual has the right to approach God for himself.

These are great doctrines I freely embrace and accept. And then the fine heritage of Baptist religious liberty— the willingness to die for the right of all people to believe as they choose. This has been a hallmark of Southern Baptist life all these years. And I am just grateful to be a part of that heritage.

VANDEMAN: I wish that all bodies, all Christian bodies, could realize the gift—the legacy of religious liberty—that you Baptists gave to them.

DRAPER: That's true. And the willingness to die for somebody else's right to believe.

VANDEMAN: That's what our program "It Is Written" is all about. We're attempting to show how God used these Reformers to rescue neglected truth for us today, and everybody benefits. But there has been a cost involved.

DRAPER: Yes. Many of our Baptist forefathers died in order to purchase religious liberty. But in America, Christianity costs so little, we don't have anything to risk. And the strength of Christianity is diluted to some degree. But our heritage is of strong sacrifice and commitment.

VANDEMAN: You would agree with me then when I say that unless we have something to die for, we probably don't have anything worth living for.

DRAPER: That's right.

VANDEMAN: Thank you, and thank God. And I'm so pleased you came.

Yes, there are so many things I like about my Baptist friends. I appreciate their emphasis on the gospel. For Baptists, you see, religion is not a theory but a Person. Baptists preach Christ and Him crucified.

I also like the Baptists' style of worship. Few things are

so inspiring as a good Baptist song service. And there's another reason I so much appreciate the Baptists. They were called by God to rescue two neglected truths—the truth about New Testament baptism, and the principle of religious liberty.

Do you realize that without our Baptists, America would probably not exist as a free nation? George Vancroft, the noted historian, observed: "Freedom of conscience, unlimited freedom of mind, was from the first the trophy of the Baptists." Our democracy, you see, was founded in the Baptist tradition of religious liberty.

Even before the days of Roger Williams, Baptists suffered much for freedom. They were born out of a complex and fascinating struggle among Protestants—a struggle for liberty of conscience.

It all started with the Anabaptist movement in sixteenth-century Europe. While Luther was pushing forward in Germany, Ulrich Zwingli launched the Swiss Reformation. Zwingli first heard the gospel while preparing for the priesthood. When called to the cathedral at Zurich in 1519, he determined to preach the good news. Spurning the prescribed sermon schedule, he opened the New Testament to his people.

Soon Zwingli met with stiff opposition. The city council, influenced by church leaders, opposed his message of salvation by faith. Yet he kept right on preaching the truth which had set him free.

But by 1523 Zwingli started backing down. During a public debate, he showed willingness to compromise. Zwingli imagined that if he toned down his reforms, he might be able to work within the system. He didn't want to alienate civic leaders. So he modified his message by seeking only a gradual reformation of church traditions.

Some of Zwingli's young students were disturbed by this. One of them, Konrad Grebel, protested that Bible truth always demands immediate action—with or without the blessing of government. Grebel became disillusioned at his teacher's willingness to accommodate the politicians. He accused Zwingli of allowing the city council to exercise authority belonging only to the Bible.

Zwingli rejected Grebel's criticism. Grebel then decided that truth must march onward even without the Reformer. With some friends, he organized home Bible study circles. Soon they rediscovered the New Testament truth about baptism.

Do you remember how the Lord Jesus was baptized? We read about it in Matthew 3:16, NIV: "As soon as Jesus was baptized, he went up out of the water."

Notice that Jesus went up out of the water after He was baptized. He had not been sprinkled or poured upon. He was submerged, immersed into the Jordan River. Believers in Christ are "buried with Him in baptism," says the apostle Paul. Colossians 2:12.

Unfortunately, the church had lost sight of this important truth. For centuries the tradition of sprinkling infants had brought everyone into the church. Now Konrad Grebel in Switzerland proclaimed that Rome and the Reformers had all been mistaken.

As you can imagine, the Zurich council did not appreciate Grebel and his group. On January 21, 1525, they passed a law prohibiting home Bible fellowships. Despite the decree, Grebel and his friends continued studying together. They determined to reject not only Rome's traditions but also Zwingli's compromises.

To seal their commitment to Christ, Grebel and his friends baptized each other again. They formed a new Christian community known as the Anabaptists— meaning those baptized twice.

How did Martin Luther react to the Anabaptists? At first the German reformer defended full freedom of con-

ANABAPTIST MEANS BAPTIZED TWICE

science. He drew a sharp distinction between church and state. Listen to what he wrote:

"Over the soul God can and will allow no one to rule but Himself alone. Therefore, where the worldly government dares to give laws to the soul, it invades the reign of God, and only seduces and corrupts the soul. This we shall make so clear that our noblemen, princes, and bishops may see what fools they are if they will force people with their laws and commandments to believe this or that."

Luther was right. Unfortunately, he came to reverse his views. What changed his mind?

It was a gradual process. During the Peasants' War, many Protestants were put to death by Catholic princes. Thousands perished on the field of battle. Luther saw the value of having government on his side instead of against him. After his teachings came to control northern Germany, Luther depended upon Protestant princes to protect the Reformation from Rome. Thus a Lutheran church-state relationship was formed.

Like Zwingli, Luther welcomed a favorable union of church and state. To them it was a matter of survival for the Reformation. But they failed to foresee the problems that always come from mixing religion and politics.

We have a similar situation in America today. Crusading to save our nation, earnest Christians are pressing hard to legislate morality. Their *own* interpretation of morality, of course. But those who have learned from the past reject religious handouts from government. They know that spiritual problems can't be solved by political action.

Notice what happened back in the sixteenth century. The Reformers had been outlawed by Rome; now they, in turn, outlawed the Anabaptists. Believe it or not, they even persecuted their fellow Christians. This is one of the most perplexing, regrettable chapters in church history.

First Zwingli urged his politician friends to crush the

nonconformists. Anabaptists in Zurich were declared under the death penalty. Later, over in Germany, Luther's associate Melanchthon argued that Anabaptists should be put to death. Even their peaceful expression of faith disrupted the religious and civil order, Melanchthon charged. He predicted that their opposition to infant baptism would produce a heathen society. Therefore they ought to be exterminated to save the nation.

Such barbarity is hard for us to accept today. Evidently Protestant leaders themselves erred, sometimes seriously. Given the weakness of human nature, we should not find this surprising. Every spiritual awakening has been marred by misguided zealots. We see in the Scriptures that even the most faithful men of God often made serious mistakes. This was also true during the Reformation.

Anabaptists were taken from their homes and thrown into prison or cruelly slain. But their blood was as seed. And those Anabaptists who escaped the sword spread their faith throughout Europe. Some went to Norway, others to Italy, Poland, Holland, and England.

Holland became a special haven for Anabaptists as well as other religious refugees. A group of British Christians fled there from their fellow Protestants in the Church of England. The two groups, Anabaptists and English Separatists, enjoyed fellowship with each other. One British pastor, John Smyth, became completely convinced by Anabaptist teachings and was rebaptized. Modern Baptists consider Smyth a pioneer of their faith.

In 1609, Smyth's group returned to England and organized the first Baptist church there. In a few years, Baptists from England came to America with their heritage of democracy and freedom. Roger Williams was only one of many Baptists who led the colonies toward liberty.

James Madison, one of America's founding fathers, was won to religious liberty by the Baptists. As a boy in Virginia he heard a fearless Baptist minister, imprisoned for his faith, preaching from the window of his cell. That day young Madison dedicated his life to fight for freedom of conscience. Tirelessly he toiled with Thomas Jefferson and others to secure the First Amendment in our Bill of Rights. It reads simply and majestically: "Congress shall make no law respecting an establishment of religion, or prohibiting the free exercise thereof."

Government, you see, must protect religion, but not promote it. Otherwise intolerance will surely raise its ugly head. History shows that whenever the religion of the majority is enforced upon society, persecution always results.

Many thoughtful Baptists are concerned these days. They are concerned that their heritage of religious freedom is fading away. They are especially sad to see some of their fellow Baptists leading the fight to legislate morality. They know that religious laws forge shackles for the soul. Persecution always comes when faith is enforced, no matter how sincere the motive may be.

Prophecies in the book of Revelation predict some unusual and distressing events in store for America. Could Puritan-style persecution arise here again? I wish we had space in this brief chapter to probe these prophecies. I urge you to write for my book *The Rise and Fall of Antichrist.* The chapter entitled "Bloodstained Stars and Stripes" contains vital information you need to know about the future of our nation.

Thank God, we still enjoy religious liberty today. How I appreciate our Baptist ancestors for bringing to America their heritage of freedom!

Now come with me back to seventeenth-century Holland. A group of Pilgrims have decided to start a colony in America. They are about to board the ship *Speedwell,* bound for the *Mayflower*. It's a time of excitement, but not without a sense of foreboding. They are leaving loved ones behind to cross the cold and unfamiliar Atlantic.

In this farewell hour, their beloved pastor John Robinson rises to speak. Listen to his words:

"Brethren, we are soon to part asunder, and the Lord only knows whether I will live to see your faces again. . . . I charge you before God to follow me no farther than I have followed Christ. If God should reveal anything to you by any other instrument of His, be as ready to receive it as you have been to receive any truth from my ministry—for I am very confident the Lord has more truth and light yet to break forth from His holy Word. . . .

"For my part, I cannot tell you how sad I am about the reformed churches. They will go no farther than the instruments of their reformation. The Lutherans cannot be drawn to go beyond what Luther saw. . . . And the Calvinists, you see, stick fast where they were left by that great man of God. . . .

"Even though these Reformers were burning and shining lights in their time, yet they did not understand all the counsel of God. But if they were living today, they would be as willing to accept further light as the light which they first received."

What a message! In these noble words we hear the true spirit of the Reformation. Willingness to learn and grow. Eagerness to walk in neglected truth that we rediscover in God's Word. Like Martin Luther at Wittenberg. Konrad Grebel in Zurich. Roger Williams at Providence. And, of course, the Methodist John Wesley in England. We will explore Wesley's fascinating ministry in our next chapter.

Today there are no oceans we haven't crossed, no more New Worlds left to discover. But new vistas of spiritual opportunity may be waiting around the corner.

Suppose God offers you new truth from His Word. Are you willing to take His hand and walk in the light? A wonderful experience awaits you!

Bishop James Ault (seated at right), president of the United Methodist Church, discussing the script with Pastor Vandeman. Bill Richards, public relations officer for the United Methodist Church, and Clara Lou Kerr, a director of communications, participate. Taped in Pittsburgh, Pennsylvania.

What I Like About the Methodists 1738

The small ship quivers, thrashed by the raging sea. Screams and splinters fill the air as the mainsail splits. Waves of terror drench the passengers. The angry Atlantic seems assured of its prey.

Amid the chaos and panic, a small group of Germans calmly sing a psalm. They seem unafraid to die. And John Wesley wonders why.

The year was 1736. Wesley, a missionary from England, barely survived his voyage to the colony of Georgia. The storm passed at last, but Wesley's soul remained in turmoil. Despite wholehearted commitment, he had somehow failed to find peace with God. What did the Germans have that he lacked?

Upon arriving in Savannah, Wesley lived for a while with the group. They were also missionaries, descendants of the fifteenth-century martyr John Huss. Fleeing persecution in their native Moravia, they had found refuge in Germany. And now they crossed the ocean to bring the gospel to the Indians.

But first a fellow Christian needed their witness. One of the Germans, looking at Wesley with kind but penetrating eyes, asked: "Do you know Christ?"

John evaded the question. "I know He is the Saviour of the world."

"Yes, but do you know He has saved *you*?"

Wesley squirmed. He had no assurance of forgiveness.

Small wonder, then, that he failed in evangelizing the Indians. After two frustrating years, Wesley returned to England.

Springtime for his soul finally blossomed in May of 1738. At a meeting in a London chapel, someone was reading from Luther's preface to his *Commentary on Romans*. Light suddenly dawned upon Wesley.

"About a quarter before nine, while he [Luther] was describing the change which God works in the heart through faith in Christ, I felt my heart strangely warmed. I felt I did trust in Christ, Christ alone for salvation; and an assurance was given me, that He had taken away my sins, even mine."

On fire with the gospel now, Wesley preached with new zeal and power. Multitudes flocked to hear him. A revival swept through England and spread to America. It was the beginning of the Methodist Church.

Methodists today are one of our major Protestant denominations. They have a world fellowship of about twenty-four million. America has some twenty Methodist bodies. The largest of them, with more than nine million members, is the United Methodist Church.

Dr. James Ault is currently president of the Council of Bishops of the United Methodist Church. We visited together recently in Pittsburgh.

VANDEMAN: Bishop James Ault, I'm so happy that you are willing to join me to represent the huge United Methodist Church and, of course, the Wesleyan tradition everywhere under your leadership.

AULT: Thank you, George. It's good to be with you today.

VANDEMAN: And also, I'd like to commend the church for its new television program, "Catch the Spirit."

AULT: We're excited about this program and have great expectations for it.

VANDEMAN: I can imagine. "Catch the Spirit"—I like that title. But now may I ask you a question? Why are you, personally, a Methodist Christian?

AULT: I was loved into the faith by my family and church school teachers, and I was loved into the ordained ministry by a pastor in our local church. But I remain a United Methodist because of its distinctive emphases. First, we're concerned about people, about human dignity and moral responsibility. Then, we've always given attention to the primacy of grace. By grace we mean the loving action of God and Jesus Christ through the activity of the Holy Spirit.

John Wesley talked about three aspects of grace. He talked about the primacy of grace—the grace that surrounds us and persuades us to move toward faith. He talked about justifying grace that has to do with a loving, accepting, pardoning God. And then growth in grace which moves us toward perfection as we mature in the faith, as we grow in grace toward sanctification—or what he would call sanctifying grace.

Then we've always been concerned about conversion— the change of heart moving people to Christ. That could happen in a dramatic way, or it could happen in a gradual way. We've always sought to keep faith and works together. And finally, our church has organized, under the Spirit, to live and to witness as the general church, combining all these local churches in one effort nationally and internationally.

VANDEMAN: That's splendidly said, and I think most Christians could subscribe to those basics. But out of these five points, what would you pick out as unique?

AULT: I think that for today, the question of faith and works. Our church has been divided into two camps since the 1960s—some giving accent to personal salvation, others to social involvement. And the church, to serve the whole gospel, must hold these together. We must grow in grace within the body and then witness, becoming the incarnation of love to the world in service.

VANDEMAN: Yes, I agree. Spiritual growth is one element that seems lacking in the emphasis of a number of groups in the Christian community. So I'm assuming you feel comfortable with our approach here in highlighting the unique features that God led the various reformers to champion—I choose to call them "neglected truths"—to bring correction to the Christian cause.

Luther rescued justification by faith, the Anabaptists brought us the principles of religious liberty and baptism by immersion. Methodists showed how conversion, followed by sanctification or growth, develops the Christian. Do you think we're handling the churches fairly?

AULT: I think it is an excellent procedure, because we share a common tradition—all of us in the Christian faith. But these distinctive emphases from church to church have enriched the whole. We share together in moving toward the whole.

VANDEMAN: Moving toward the whole. How right you are! Thank you so much, Jim. We appreciate your coming.

AULT: Thank you.

There are many things I like about my Methodist friends. I appreciate their historic stand on sober and disciplined living. I admire their organized church government. I salute their concern for the handicapped and for social outcasts. I enjoy Methodist music. Some of my favorite hymns were written by Charles Wesley, John's brother.

Let me say it again—there are so many things I like about our Methodist friends. But there's one thing I especially appreciate: the Methodist movement was called by God to rescue a neglected truth. Wesley stressed that Christians will yield the fruit of obedience as the result of their relationship with Christ.

You remember that Luther restored a neglected truth as well—salvation by faith alone. And John Calvin proclaimed the good news that salvation comes directly from God, not from the church. This also had been a neglected truth. Then the Anabaptists came along to champion truth that had been forgotten. So it was also with Wesley. He brought a necessary balance to the teachings of John Calvin and Martin Luther.

By the eighteenth century, England had backslidden from God. Wesley's preaching jolted the nation out of its spiritual slumber. Of course, not everyone appreciated the awakening. Trapped in the cobwebs of tradition, the churches closed their doors against the new Reformer. So Wesley took to the fields. He preached outdoors, at sunrise, before workers began their daily toil.

Listen to his diary entry from September 21, 1743: "I was wakened between 3 and 4 a.m. by a large company of tinners, who, fearing they should be too late, had gathered round the house, and were singing and praising God. At five I preached once more, on, 'Believe on the Lord Jesus Christ, and thou shalt be saved.' They all devoured the word."

Converts crowded Wesley's meetings. He tried to keep his movement within the established church. But most of his recruits had been unchurched, so Wesley organized them into societies to provide for their spiritual care. Even so, he insisted they attend regular Church of England services.

But in spite of Wesley's loyalty to the official church, the religious and civil authorities rejected his ministry. And Wesley suffered more than mere refusal of his right to preach. On July 4, 1745, a mob smashed into his house and demanded his death. Listen as he describes the experience:

"I stepped forward at once into the midst of them, and said, 'Here I am. Which of you has anything to say to me? To which of you have I done any wrong? To you? Or you? Or you?' I continued speaking till I came . . . into the middle of the street, and then raising my voice, said, 'Neighbors, countrymen! Do you desire to hear me speak?' They cried vehemently, 'Yes, Yes. He shall speak. He shall. Nobody shall hinder him.' . . . I spoke . . . till one or two of their [mob] captains turned about and swore, [that] not a man should touch [me]."

Sometimes opposition to Wesley backfired, as his diary in September of 1769 recorded:

"Then they lifted up their voice [against me], especially one, called a gentleman, who had filled his pocket with rotten eggs; but, a young man coming unawares, clapped his hands on each side, and mashed them all at once. In an instant he was perfume all over; though it was not so sweet as balsam."

Never a dull moment for John Wesley! And never an idle moment either. He rode on horseback a quarter of a million miles in his ministry. For more than half a century he averaged at least fifteen sermons a week.

Let's visit the place where so many of those sermons

were written. Wesley's house still stands today in London. I've visited it on several occasions.

In front of the window in Wesley's prayer room is a table with a kneeling bench and chair. And on the table just two things—Wesley's Greek New Testament and a candle. Every morning at four Wesley came into this little room to kneel down and talk to God. This was the power place of Methodism.

Near the end of Wesley's long and faithful life he wrote:

"I am now an old man, decayed from head to foot. My eyes are dim; my right hand shakes much; my mouth is hot and dry every morning; I have a lingering fever almost every day; my motion is weak and slow. However, blessed be God, I do not slack my labor: I can preach and write still."

Wesley's long ministry centered on two great truths which had been overlooked: God's forgiveness is free to everyone, and all of us are responsible to trust and obey.

May I show you a chart that illustrates Wesley's message? Illustrations, of course, have their weaknesses. There's no way to exactly chart the delicate work of the Holy Spirit. But illustrations can clarify spiritual truth. Jesus, you know, used parables to explain His teaching.

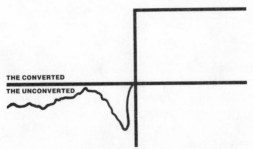

PERFECTION OR MATURITY IN JESUS

THE CONVERTED

THE UNCONVERTED

Let's say this chart represents my life. The line across the center stands for my conversion. All activity above the line follows conversion. Below the line traces my life before my new birth. The line at the top represents perfection—perfection as seen in the life of Jesus. And the wavy line running across the chart traces my daily experience.

Notice my life before conversion. I'm trying to be a good family man and respectable citizen. I work hard. I pay my taxes. I'm kind to my loved ones—I may even go to church. But I'm still unconverted. I'm not yet ready to accept Jesus as my Saviour and my Lord.

But I am considering a change. Starting at the left side of the chart, you see me edging toward conversion, toward exchanging my old ways for a new life in Jesus. Perhaps a Christian television program has drawn me toward surrendering to Christ. Maybe a tragedy like losing a loved one has shown me my need of God. Or even something wonderful like becoming a parent has made me want to be a Christian.

So here I am, about to commit my life to Christ. But then I draw back, reluctant to exchange some of my old ways for the way God wants me to live.

For a while I waver back and forth, trying to decide what to do. Fighting conviction, I find myself dropping deeper into sin. But the devil oversteps himself in his temptations. I read the fine print in his contract and realize he intends to bring about my ruin. Alarmed, I turn to Jesus as my refuge. I now realize why He died for me, and I can no longer resist His love.

So at last I unreservedly surrender myself to Him as my Saviour. By an act of God I now experience what is frequently called "being born again." A happy experience indeed. But at this crucial moment, please notice the chart. I immediately face what seems to be an impossible challenge—perfection of character. How can I ever reach it?

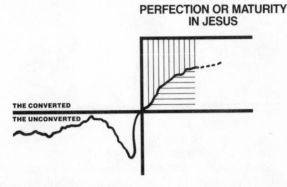

PERFECTION OR MATURITY IN JESUS

But notice: since I am forgiven, at that very moment I stand clean before God, perfect in His sight. The Saviour has given me the record of His holy life—it's just as if I had never sinned. Undeserving though I am, God treats me as if I were at the top of the chart. In theological terms, this is called justification.

But as for my daily living, I've just begun the Christian life. I'm a spiritual babe, you see. Babies need to grow, and I must too.

So I begin a relationship with Jesus that replaces my relationship with sin. On the chart, below the wavy line, you see the record of how much I am permitting Christ to live out His live in me.

But does the record of this progress complete the requirement of perfection or maturity in Christ? No. However, if I am walking in all the light He sends me and remain committed to Him, moment by moment, He makes up the difference by giving me the record of His own perfect life, and I stand justified in His sight.

But suppose I become perplexed. Old temptations return again and again to attack me. And sometimes I find myself yielding on the spur of the moment. Does this mean I'm not saved?

Not at all. Babies have their falls, you know. My little grandson Craig gets bumped so many times I wonder how he manages to keep smiling. And when he learns to walk, he will often stumble. But he'll get back up again. And all the time he is growing!

So it is with the Christian life. Along with the many victories God gives me, I find myself stumbling at times. But then by His grace I am able to get back on my feet.

But as long as I'm willing to permit Christ to live out His life within me, I remain forgiven. The perfection of the Saviour, you see, covers my shortcomings. When God looks at me, He doesn't see my weaknesses—He sees Jesus, His Son. He credits me with Christ's perfect life. So God can say about me, "This is My beloved son or daughter, in whom I am well pleased."

Do you see the good news here? At every level of Christian growth, God considers us perfect. And if you think that is an overstatment, consider a baby. Babies are perfect in every stage of development, are they not?

That's what God means by the word *perfect,* or mature. And all the while God counts us perfect—or mature—in Christ, He is drawing us closer and closer to becoming like Jesus.

Now, suppose I die. I still have shortcomings. I still have growth that I have not yet realized. Does this mean I am lost?

Of course not—the perfect record of Jesus still covers me. I remain forgiven in God's sight because, as God's Word says: "If we walk in the light as He is in the light . . . the blood of Jesus Christ His Son cleanses us from all sin." 1 John 1:7.

Thrilling news! Constant cleansing *if* we walk in the light of His Word.

PERFECTION OR MATURITY
IN JESUS

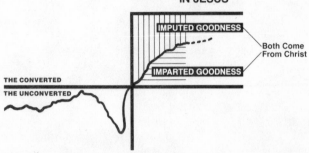

So now as we summarize the meaning of the right half of this chart, remember that illustrations have their weaknesses. But notice how this helps. Everything below the wavy line is the record of God's *imparted* goodness—Christ living in my life. And everything above the line is God's *imputed* goodness—Christ's perfect record covering my life. Both, you see, come from Christ.

The imputed righteousness of Jesus is an umbrella that covers me with forgiveness as long as I live. I don't outgrow my need for justification, that is, my need to be covered by the blood of Jesus. Yet all the time I am forgiven, of course, I am also growing in sanctification, Christ's imparted righteousness. God in this wonderful and encouraging way is working in us to restore the image of our Maker.

This was the message of salvation that warmed the heart of Wesley. This is the neglected truth he restored to give balance to our faith.

Can you see why I like the Methodists? God had called Luther and Calvin to proclaim forgiveness. Then He brought Wesley on the scene to stress clean living and

Christian growth. All of them brought back vital truths that had been neglected.

Of course, John Wesley did not claim to have all the light himself. He knew that as long as time would last, new truths would unfold from God's Word.

Have you ever wondered why we have so many denominations? Maybe you have begun to see the answer in these past several chapters. We tend to follow our leaders—to believe everything they believe but little more. To advance no farther than they do before they die. To draw a circle around their teachings and form a creed.

Now, creeds have expressed in profound language the roots of the Christian faith and have also provided a convenient way for expressing our beliefs. But they can unfortunately lock us into a particular set of teachings and keep us from following newly rediscovered truth. We find refuge in our heritage, and that is fine up to a point. But then we tend to dig in our heels. We refuse to advance past the boundary of our established beliefs.

Can you see how this has happened in the history of the church? When God introduced advanced light—neglected truth—in the days of Luther, the Catholic Church refused it. So the Lutheran Church was born. When God brought more light with the Anabaptists, most Lutherans did not accept it. The Baptist Church emerged. And when additional truth came through Wesley, many Calvinists and others turned him down. So we have the Methodists. The story goes on and on.

Will it ever end? We shall see.

Let me give you something to think about. Is it possible that there may be advanced light for *us* to follow? Neglected truths from God's Word we need to follow today—whatever our denominational ties? The Bible says: "The path of the just is as the shining light, that shineth more and more unto the perfect day." Proverbs 4:18, KJV.

But many people seem to be reluctant to welcome new light, unlike a little girl in colonial New England who had caught the spirit of Wesley. She penned a little poem which a circuit-riding preacher copied in his diary. May I share it with you? Believe it or not, the girl who wrote this poem was just nine years old. Listen to her message:

> Know then that every soul is free,
>   To choose his life and what he'll be.
> For this eternal truth is given,
>   That God will force no man to heaven.
>
> He'll draw, persuade, direct him right,
>   Bless him with wisdom, love, and light.
> In nameless ways be good and kind,
>   But never force the human mind.

Yes, friend, God will never force the human mind. You and I are free. Free to do whatever we will as truth goes marching on. We can refuse to grow beyond the beliefs of our ancestors. Or we can choose for ourselves to walk in the light that continually shines from the inexhaustible Word of God.

God help us to make the right choice!

Demos Shakarian, president of the Full Gospel Businessmen's Fellowship International, speaks with his longtime friend, George Vandeman, in Los Angeles. Mr. Shakarian, a businessman, is one of the most visible representatives of the Charismatic movement today.

What I Like About the Charismatics

Something big is happening. Something that we've never seen before. A Charismatic revival is sweeping across America.

It's changing churches. It's changing people. Should it be changing you?

It all began in California back in April 1960. Dennis Bennett, rector of St. Mark's Episcopal Church in Van Nuys, confronted his congregation with a startling announcement. And Christianity has never been the same since.

Bennett informed his people that the previous October he had received the "baptism of the Holy Spirit." He testified, "The Holy Spirit did take my lips and tongue and form a powerful language . . . that I myself could not understand."

Bennett's sophisticated church was shocked. One of his associates resigned on the spot and stalked out. Many exited with him.

But multitudes since then have had a spiritual experience like Bennett's. Huge "Jesus rallies" pack football stadiums. Testimonies of changed lives ring through the air amid fervent Hallelujahs. Tears of joy stream down beaming faces. Arm and arm together, Protestants and Catholics sing "We Are One in the Spirit."

No doubt about it, something big is happening. According to a recent Gallup poll, nearly thirty million Americans in scores of denominations call themselves Charismatics. Many consider this awakening the greatest religious event since the first-century Pentecost. Others are not so sure.

What's really going on?

To understand this Charismatic revival, we must go back to the days of the early Methodists. John Wesley taught that after believers are born again, a "still higher salvation" awaits them. He called this experience the "second blessing" of the Holy Spirit. It would come suddenly, Wesley said, instantly cleansing and renewing the soul. Sin would be replaced by perfect love.

Wesley and his preachers urged their audiences to seek the ultimate outpouring of the Spirit. Interestingly, Wesley himself never claimed to have attained his second blessing. But he sought the experience until his death.

After Wesley passed from the scene, various leaders continued to promote his second blessing. Prominent among them was Phoebe Palmer, who published a *Guide to Christian Perfection*. In it she suggested that entire holiness is not won by spiritual struggle, but by trustfully claiming God's promises. She called this experience the baptism of the Holy Spirit.

Despite the efforts of many revivalists, by the mid-nineteenth century the Methodist Church was losing its first love. Seeking spiritual renewal, holiness societies abounded. One such group inspired Hannah Whitall Smith to write *The Christian's Secret of a Happy Life*. We'll talk more about that devotional classic later.

Many holiness revivalists promoted a Pentecost-style religion that majored in miracles. Believing themselves under direct guidance by the Holy Spirit, they resisted the restraints of church authority. Finally the Methodist

PENTECOST — A CHRISTIAN FESTIVAL CELEBRATED ON THE 7TH SUNDAY after EASTER COMMEMORATING THE DECENT OF THE HOLY SPIRIT UPON APOSTLES.

Church felt forced to disavow the holiness movement.

So the Pentecostals flourished outside of Methodism. Within just a few years around the turn of the century, more than twenty holiness groups were born. The largest of them were the Nazarenes and the Pilgrim Holiness Church. Later the various Churches of God appeared, and other denominations too.

Many holiness believers began speaking in tongues. Charles Fox Parham, a faith healer in Topeka, Kansas, sparked this tongues revival. Parham urged speaking in tongues as a necessary experience for every Christian.

Soon Pentecostal fires lit Los Angeles, scene of the famous Azusa Street revival in 1906. Tongues became the heartbeat of religion for many holiness denominations. But mainline Protestants and the Catholics shunned Pentecostalism.

Then came the 1960s when everything changed. After Dennis Bennett took his stand at St. Marks, barriers crumbled between Pentecostals and their fellow Protestants. Eager believers from scores of denominations began to talk in tongues. This new interfaith movement became known as the Charismatic renewal.

Before long, some Catholics joined the ranks of Charismatics. In June of 1967, ninety Catholics gathered at Notre Dame to celebrate their new tongues experience. Just seven years later, the group had swelled to 35,000. Charismatic growth among Catholics has been remarkable—almost incredible. A recent poll showed that four million American Catholics attended a Charismatic meeting within the month they were surveyed.

How do Catholic leaders feel about tongues? Pope Paul VI unofficially but unmistakably blessed the Charismatic revival. And early in 1981, Pope John Paul II expressed explicit appreciation for the Charismatic renewal within the church.

Many Catholic scholars have endorsed tongues. Edward O'Conner wrote, "Catholics who have accepted Pentecostal spirituality have found it to be fully in harmony with their traditional faith and life."

Many lay people have become involved in interfaith Charismatic groups. The largest and best known of them is the Full Gospel Businessmen's Fellowship International. Recently it was my privilege to converse with a cherished friend of many years—Demos Shakarian, the founder and president of that group.

VANDEMAN: Demos, I wish you could know how pleased I am to have you with me today.

SHAKARIAN: And I'm extremely happy to be with you, George. I have always considered you one of my best friends.

VANDEMAN: Twenty years of friendship.

SHAKARIAN: And I've been watching your telecast, "It Is Written," for many years, George. What a blessing you've been to me personally—and to thousands of my friends. Your program is known all over the nation.

VANDEMAN: Thank you. I need your prayers, Demos. Tell us something about your background. You're not a minister. Your leadership has not been in the ministry. You're a lay person—a businessman. And you have gathered around you multiplied thousands of business people in your fellowship.

SHAKARIAN: Yes, we started with twenty-one men at Clifton's Cafeteria in Los Angeles. Today we have over 800,000, and they meet every month in eighty-seven countries and 4,000 chapters. God is blessing through the power of the Holy Spirit.

VANDEMAN: I think our viewers can understand why I chose you to speak for the Charismatic movement. You're known everywhere—known among the high and the low. Talking your faith with presidents. But may I ask you this, Demos, Why are you a Charismatic Christian?

SHAKARIAN: That's where the power is. The baptism of the Holy Spirit. That's the same power the disciples had in the upper room when 3,000 were saved in one day and 5,000 another day. And Peter raised the dead and healed the sick. He didn't do it on his own. He did it by the power of the Holy Spirit. I know that's what the men want to see, a reality of Christianity—the Charismatic movement.

VANDEMAN: The Holy Spirit needs to be talked about and received more than any other gift, wouldn't you say?

SHAKARIAN: I would say so.

VANDEMAN: Now, you have read all I'm going to say in this telecast, which will also be in the book. Do you feel that I've treated the Charismatic movement fairly?

SHAKARIAN: You've done a beautiful job, right from the heart. I was really proud of you. I thought, "There's my friend, George Vandeman."

VANDEMAN: Thank you. We want to build bridges, and we also want to frankly share cautions. But you feel I have been fair?

SHAKARIAN: Yes, I like it very much. I approve it.

Yes, there is so much I appreciate about my Charismatic friends. I like their warmth, their love, and their enthusiasm—as noted by Demos. Charismatics have contributed so much to the spontaneity and joy of worship. And in this age of secular self-sufficiency, they remind us that we are dependent beings—dependent upon God's Spirit in order to fulfill the purpose of our lives.

Another thing I like about Charismatics is their prayer experience. When they pray, they really pray! And they expect answers from their Father in heaven.

Let me say it again, there are so many things I appreciate about the Charismatics. In fact, I'm a Charismatic myself, in the biblical sense of the word. Let me explain. The word *charismatic* in Greek means "gift of grace." And I believe in the gifts of the Spirit. So I am a Charismatic. But I don't speak in tongues.

Now this creates a question for many Charismatics. You see, they believe that tongues is the proof of the Holy Spirit's presence. Unless I talk in tongues, I'm somehow underprivileged. Maybe a second-class Christian. Some would probably even say that because I can't speak in tongues, I'm not saved at all. Now I don't hold that against them. And they don't hold it against me. They just worry about me.

But let me set their minds at rest. There are many different gifts of the Spirit. The Bible never says everyone receives the same gift. Jesus had the power of the Spirit as no other ever had it or ever will. John the Baptist said of Him, "To him God gives the Spirit without limit." John 3:34, NIV. Yet there is no record indicating that Jesus ever talked in tongues. That's something to think about, isn't it?

What is the purpose of tongues? Well, the apostles used tongues to communicate the gospel in a foreign language. The word translated "tongue" really means "language," you see. When Christ sent the apostles to evangelize the world, He didn't want them to have to spend years taking language classes. So He gave them the gift of tongues, and thousands from all over heard the gospel in their own languages at Pentecost.

There's another gift Charismatics mention much—the gift of healing. You've noticed faith healers on television. They tell us God wants to heal all sickness as soon as we have faith. Now, I certainly believe in healing. But the guarantee of instant healing may not turn out to be such good news after all—it can create a tremendous load of guilt.

Let me explain. If faith ought always to bring healing, then those who remain ill must not have faith. The sick are somehow not "spiritual" enough to be healed.

This type of thinking gets more serious. Listen: If the faith that saves me ought to heal me, then when I'm not healed, maybe I'm not saved. Can you see the potential for a problem here? Many dying saints cry to God to be healed, yet they remain sick. So they come to doubt their salvation. They carry a false burden of guilt even worse than their pain.

Now, as I've said, I believe in divine healing. Many we have prayed for at "It Is Written" have been miraculously healed. But I've also seen many saints die from disease. You have too, haven't you? And the Lord loves them just the same as if He healed them now.

You see, God wants to heal us in His own time and way, as He knows best. Sometimes He heals immediately. Sometimes gradually. And sometimes He waits to heal us until the resurrection when Jesus comes.

The apostle Paul believed in healing. He even raised a young man from death. But he himself was never healed of a mysterious affliction called his "thorn in the flesh." Three times he begged God for deliverance. Finally he accepted this suffering. It was a blessing, to keep him humble and dependent. So he committed his affliction to God and went on with life.

Let me ask you. Does it take more faith to demand to be healed now—or to commit your body to God and let Him heal it when He knows is best? Tell me, which takes more faith—to get what I want now, or to let God work in His time and way?

Thank God, salvation does not depend upon whether or not we get a particular answer to prayer. Instead, being saved depends upon whether we decide to trust and obey Jesus. Our hope rests in Christ, not in ourselves. Jesus is our ticket to heaven.

Suppose we could earn salvation on the basis of having miracles in our lives. That would put us in competition with Jesus, our Saviour—wouldn't it? But our faith must *accept* Christ, not *compete* with Him. We look away from ourselves to the cross. So we are saved through the blood of Jesus, not by the miracles God works in our lives.

Misunderstanding miracles can lead to all kinds of spiritual problems. I'm reminded of one poor man with an up-and-down Christian experience. He confesses to spiritual pride when he sees remarkable answers to his prayers. But when nothing much happens, he gets worried that God has abandoned him. He fears he might be lost. This man must learn to look away from himself—away from anything happening in his life. He needs to put his trust outside of himself in Jesus.

Now, as I mentioned before, I believe in miracles. And I welcome all the gifts of the Spirit. God will work wonders in our lives if we cooperate with Him. But when we put our trust in the cross of Christ, we will never make a savior out of our spiritual accomplishments.

Do you see what I mean? Let's think this through further. Suppose I feel assured of salvation just because I see miracles happening in my life. I might become careless in my obedience, you see. One Charismatic actually wrote on the flyleaf of his Bible: "I don't care what the Bible says, I've had an experience."

It is not our place to question the sincerity of this man. But surely the Holy Spirit, who inspired the Bible, would never lead us to neglect obeying God's Word. Could this be why the Bible brings us a warning in 1 John 4:1? Listen: "Do not believe every spirit, but test the spirits, whether they are of God."

Important advice, wouldn't you say? Evidently enemy spirits can counterfeit the Holy Spirit. They can work real miracles, even causing fire to come down from heaven in a false Pentecost. See Revelation 13:13, 14. And the Scriptures actually predict that the enemy will perform his evil wonders using the name of Jesus Christ. Listen to these words from Jesus Himself: "Many will say to Me in that day, 'Lord, Lord, have we not prophesied in Your name, cast out demons in Your name, and done many wonders in Your name?' And then I will declare to them, 'I never knew you; depart from Me, you who practice lawlessness.' " Matthew 7:22, 23.

So false prophets will use Christ's name to practice lawlessness. Satan will perform all kinds of lying wonders. He can abuse the gift of healing in the name of Jesus. And he can counterfeit the gift of tongues. After all, he is an angel fallen. He can speak any language of earth or heaven.

Never forget it—miracles themselves are certainly not proof of God's presence. Evidently some miracles could be the work of the enemy!

Do you see why the Bible warns us to try the spirits? And what is the test? How can I tell genuine love for God from its counterfeit? Scripture says, "This is the love of God, that we keep His commandments. And His commandments are not burdensome." 1 John 5:3.

You see, love for God means far more than a feeling that warms our hearts when we worship. The true test of Christian love is obedience. Obedience to God's commandments.

Friend, please let me warn you with all my heart—beware. And I know Demos Shakarian and his associates would agree with me when I tell you this: watch out for counterfeits of the Holy Spirit. Keep your eyes open—and your Bible close by!

Now that I've shared these cautions, again let me pour out my heart. Too many of us are satisfied with a humdrum experience, lacking the fire of the Holy Spirit in our lives. God wants us to have more. So much more! He wants to fill our hearts with love. To bring us victory over sin. To guide us into all truth.

The Holy Spirit is God's greatest gift—and our greatest need. So let's ask God to fill our lives to overflowing with His true Spirit. Then we ought to let the Spirit decide what gift to give us. Don't you think?

And now as we near the close of this chapter, may I share with you a story? You remember earlier I mentioned Hannah Whithall Smith and her book *The Christian's Secret of a Happy Life*. There is an interesting background behind her experience. I learned of it from Catherine Marshall's book *Something More*.

In 1865 Hannah and her husband Robert moved their family to Milltown, New Jersey. That's where Hannah encountered the holiness Methodists. Even though she was a Quaker, she was profoundly influenced by them.

Soon Robert came to share his wife's interest in holy living. One summer they attended a holiness camp meeting at a wooded campsite along the New Jersey coast. Robert, but not Hannah, received a sensational spiritual experience. Here's how she later described what happened to him:

"After the meeting my husband had gone alone into a spot in the woods to continue to pray by himself. Suddenly, from head to foot he was shaken with what seemed like a magnetic thrill of heavenly delight, and floods of glory seemed to pour through him, soul and body, with the inward assurance that this was the longed-for Baptism of the Holy Spirit."

Well, naturally this made Hannah desire a similar experience. She went to the altar night after night. She prayed for hours on end. But nothing happened. Not then or ever did she have a spectacular spiritual experience such as had come to her husband.

At first she was disappointed. Then she realized that God had already given her His Spirit in the peace that reigned in her heart. She had something more permanent and substantial than a dramatic and sensational experience.

But the story isn't over. In the spring of 1875 Robert traveled to Germany, where he held highly successful evangelistic and teaching meetings before large crowds, always in a highly-charged emotional atmosphere. In a letter to his wife he exulted, "All Europe is at my feet!" When engraved pictures of him were offered for sale, 8,000 sold immediately.

Then the bottom fell out of Robert's ministry. Gossip circulated about his questionable conduct with the ladies. Rumors hit the press. Meetings were canceled by sponsors. Robert returned home to Hannah.

Hannah faithfully stood by her husband, quietly supporting him. And what about Robert and his sensational spiritual experience? His faith failed. He sank into the depths of depression. But through it all, Hannah continued in her quiet, consistent Christianity. Don't you admire her faithfulness?

Friend, let's let God come into our lives in any way He

chooses. He may not come to us with the gifts of healing or tongues. He may, in fact, come with a leash for our tongues. Or He may quietly convict us of new truth that we've never known before. Neglected truth for us to follow.

But in one way or another, He will come into our lives when we surrender ourselves in faith. And we don't need to wait for some kind of sensational experience. The quiet infilling of your life by the Holy Spirit can be yours just now.

> Spirit of the living God,
>   Fall afresh on me!
> Break me, melt me, mold me, fill me.
>   Spirit of the living God,
> Fall afresh on me!

Dr. Samuele Bacchiocchi visiting with Pastor Vandeman in Washington, D. C., just prior to the television taping of his statement on the Catholic Church.

What I Like About the Catholics

It's nineteen minutes past five. The little white Pope-mobile circles St. Peter's Square in Rome amid the waving, cheering crowd.

Nobody notices a flight bag being unzipped. Nobody sees the hand reaching inside or the black Browning pistol pulled out.

Then it happens. Sudden gunfire erupts, and the smiling man in white grimaces in pain. His broad shoulders sway and slowly collapse.

Cheers turn to screams. In a dozen languages the awful news ripples through the crowd: "The pope has been shot!"

Bright red blood spurts from a gaping wound. The race for life toward Gemelli Hospital is a scene of deepening horror. Deathly pale and barely conscious, John Paul murmurs, "Why did they do it?"

Multiplied millions repeat the anguished question, the angry demand, "Why?" Prayers ascend from everywhere as priests, pastors, and rabbis lead their congregations in fervent intercession for the pope.

John Paul recovered and returned to the open arms of three quarters of a billion Catholics. His worldwide crusade for friendship and peace moved forward.

What is it about John Paul that wins hearts everywhere? I think we all appreciate his friendly, warm-hearted style.

Not so long ago, you recall, the Western world had been flirting with unrestrained freedom. Society in the sixties began following a different drummer. "Doing your own thing." And it was all in the name of peace and love.

But this erosion of morality swept us into the gutter of pain and shame. We suffered the heartache of teenage pregnancy, drinking, and drug addiction. Not to mention vandalism, violence, and venereal disease. All this stemmed from rejecting God's standard of moral absolutes, His Ten Commandments.

America finally came to its senses. The late seventies brought a revival of morality, when many who had rejected God's law changed their minds. They came to realize that social action can never take the place of spiritual values. And as for the different drummer society had been following—they wondered if the drummer was mad!

In this atmosphere of religious renewal, John Paul became pope. He quickly filled a void in moral leadership. Who could ever forget his visit to the United States in the fall of 1979? He arrived in the rain at Boston's airport and announced: "To all I have come with a message of hope and peace—the hope and peace of Jesus Christ."

That evening in Boston Commons, John Paul had special counsel for America's youth: "Faced with problems and disappointments," he said, many young people "escape from their responsibility, escape in selfishness, escape in sexual pleasure, escape in drugs, escape in violence, escape in indifference and cynical attitudes. But today I propose to you the option of love, which is the opposite of escape."

John Paul continued: "Real love is demanding. I would fail in my mission if I did not tell you so. For it was Jesus—our Lord Jesus Himself—who said: 'You are my friends if you do what I command you.' "

Many thought the youth might reject the pope's call to spiritual law and order. But no, 19,000 teenagers at Madison Square Garden the next day clapped and cheered as he urged them to discipline their lives. They were ready for the challenging morality of Pope John Paul.

So were the rest of America's more than fifty million Catholics. You remember how 80,000 packed Yankee Stadium to hear the pontiff. An avalanche of applause followed when the pope admonished them to share with the poor and oppressed.

John Paul's appeals for morality and compassion touched hearts wherever he went. And Americans of all religious persuasions appreciated his call to social and spiritual responsibility.

Now, you have noticed that in previous chapters I have asked leaders of the various denominations to help us get acquainted with their churches and to tell of their personal faith in Christ. I found leaders of the Catholic Church warm and friendly, pleased that their church would be included in this book. But they were reticent to appear publicly. So I turned to Dr. Samuele Bacchiocchi. Although not of the Catholic faith, he was the only non-Catholic ever accepted as a graduate student in the famed Pontifical Gregorian University. After five years of study there in Rome, he was awarded the highest honor the pontiff can give a graduate—the gold medal of scholarly achievement. We talked together in Washington, D.C:

VANDEMAN: Dr. Bacchiocchi, this is going to be interesting. Welcome to our program today.

BACCHIOCCHI: Thank you, George.

VANDEMAN: From your unique background, Sam, what do you like about the Roman Catholic people themselves?

BACCHIOCCHI: I can think of several things which I really appreciate about Catholic people. On a personal level, what I like is the way they treated me during those five years I spent in Rome at the Pontifical Gregorian University. They enrolled me as a "separated brother," but in reality they treated me as a real Christian brother, with love, respect, and kindness.

In a more general way, what I like about Catholics is their dedication to their religious exercises. I was privileged while studying at the Vatican University to observe my professors, priests, and monks spending the early hours of the day in reading and meditation. The impact of their daily communion with God could really be seen in their piety and pleasant disposition.

I also greatly admire the sacrificial spirit of countless priests and monks—and nuns like Mother Teresa. Through personal sacrifice they serve the needy, the suffering, the forgotten of our society.

VANDEMAN: I agree with you 100 percent. Now, what do you like about Catholic teaching?

BACCHIOCCHI: Well, first of all, as a Protestant there are several Catholic teachings that you can understand my finding unacceptable, such as transubstantiation, the immaculate conception, and so on. On the other hand, however, other Catholic teachings I not only admire, but believe are very relevant to our time. I'm thinking particularly of the Roman Catholic commitment to preserve the sacredness of marriage. They cherish the sanctity of human life.

We live in a society where many Christians have come to view marriage as a secular social institution that can be readily dissolved when circumstances call for it. The Catholic Church has to be commended for reminding us

● TRANSUBSTANTIATION —(IN THE EUCHARIST)
THE CONVERSION OF THE WHOLE SUBSTANCE OF THE
BREAD and WINE INTO THE BODY and BLOOD OF CHRIST
ONLY THE EXTERNAL APPEARANCE OF BREAD and WINE
REMAINING.

that marriage is sacred and that what God has united no one has the right to put asunder.

I also greatly admire the efforts of the Catholic Church since Vatican II to promote the circulation and reading of the Word of God. I believe, George, that this is a very positive development that can greatly help believers enrich their experience of spiritual life. My fervent hope and prayer is that we as Protestants might come to appreciate more fully the religious experience of our Catholic friends. And on the other hand, that our Catholic friends, through renewed study of the Scriptures, might come to rediscover some of these lost but vital biblical truths.

VANDEMAN: And who could have said it better than you? Thank you for coming.

There is so much I personally appreciate about the Catholics. In a world of material progress and social change, moral values have eroded—but the Roman Catholic Church stands for morality and decency. And most Catholics honor the sanctity of human life, along with many conservative Protestants who recognize respect for life as a neglected truth. These convictions have through the years made America great, and Catholics have been an important part of the moral fiber of this nation. The Catholic Church has continued to stand firm, even while others have slipped.

I also like Catholics because of their many radiant examples of genuine Christian love. A self-forgetful love asking nothing in return—the kind of love Jesus showed in His life. One favorite illustration of this, as Dr. Bacchiocchi reminded us, is Mother Teresa of Calcutta, India. Where is the heart so hard that it is not touched and challenged to its depths by what this dear woman is doing? And let us not forget that there are thousands of other nuns and priests like Mother Teresa in all corners of the world. Not until eternity will we know the sacrifices of these unsung heroes.

Something else I appreciate about Catholics is their sincere love for Jesus and their growing interest in the Scriptures. I witnessed this firsthand in Cardinal Kroll of Philadelphia when we worked together under the honorary leadership of President Reagan during the recent Year of the Bible. The church council Vatican II, back in the sixties, encouraged members to read God's Word. And some of the finest biblical research today is being done by Catholic scholars.

Now you understand that I am not a Roman Catholic. So there are differences between my beliefs and those of the Catholic Church. And that's to be expected and understood, of course. Probably the most basic difference between us is the matter of papal infallibility and the role of tradition in interpreting Scripture, as a foundation of spiritual authority.

But I've noticed something in recent years since Vatican II. A trend has developed among many Catholic scholars and informed laypeople—a trend of going back to Scripture as the basis of belief. Of course, they recognize the prominent role tradition has played in the past. But as I say, now there is a movement among Catholic people to more fully establish their roots in Scripture. And we must commend them for that trend.

Church traditions may change over the years, but the Word of God remains the same. This is another reason why more and more Catholic people are coming to recognize the importance of the Bible.

Could this be the message we get from the apostle Paul's visit to Berea? Berea of ancient Macedonia is presently the city of Veroia in the nation of Greece. You can imagine how happy the Bereans were to have Paul's ministry.

They may have even cheered when he came to town. And they eagerly listened to everything he had to say.

But the Bereans scrutinized Paul's teaching. And you know, the apostle didn't mind a bit! Notice: "The Bereans were of more noble character than the Thessalonians, for they received the message with great eagerness and examined the Scriptures every day to see if what Paul said was true." Acts 17:11, NIV.

The apostle Paul, you see, invited the church to evaluate what he taught them. He wanted them to prove it for themselves in the Scriptures before they accepted his teaching. So the Bereans weren't being disloyal for checking everything Paul said by the Bible. In fact, they were called noble.

Tell me. Does the test that the apostle Paul applied to his own teachings pertain to church leaders and Bible teachers today? Please don't take anything I say as truth just because I say it, no matter how sincere I may be. Check everything by God's Word.

Even though I have some basic differences with the Roman Catholic Church in interpreting the Bible, let me say this once again: I appreciate the reverence so many Catholics have for the sacred Scriptures—much more, I must admit, than some Protestant liberals who reject the virgin birth of Jesus and what I believe are other fundamentals of faith. We should also remember that every Catholic catechism teaches obedience to God's law. But have you ever noticed the difference in the Ten Commandments as taught by the Church of Rome and the Ten Commandments we find in the Bible? See Exodus 20:3-17.

Notice in their catechisms that the second commandment is missing. That's the one discouraging the use of images in worship. Evidently this commandment created a problem in the light of church teaching. So it was removed entirely in these catechisms. But, you ask, how does the church still count Ten Commandments? Well, it divides the tenth commandment into two so it still can keep ten.

Right here we must be careful to be fair. Let's not misunderstand the use of images by our Catholic friends. They don't worship the images themselves, which they well know are only statues of wood and stone. They honor the lives of the saints represented by these images.

You see, Catholics believe certain saints walked so closely with God that their characters became holy. And now, through the merits of these saints, they teach, imperfect Christians can approach God.

Now I understand that the second commandment does not permit such enshrinement of saints. Because all humans, even the best of us, fall short of God's ideal. Yet there's good news—all who believe and obey the gospel are accounted as saints. This means we all can approach God on our own through the blood of Christ. So many Catholics have come to believe that all Christians are equally perfect in God's sight through Jesus.

Let's take a look at what happened to the fourth commandment, which is listed as third in the Catholic catechism. This is the Sabbath commandment, and it has been changed too. This may be a surprising revelation to some, but the Roman Catholic Church freely informs us of their influence in that change from Sabbath to Sunday. We read about it in *The Convert's Catechism of Catholic Doctrine* (1977 ed., p. 50):

Q. Which is the Sabbath day?
A. Saturday is the Sabbath day.
Q. Why do we observe Sunday instead of Saturday?
A. We observe Sunday instead of Saturday because the Catholic Church transferred the solemnity from Saturday to Sunday.

Interesting, wouldn't you say? There's a fascinating history behind this thinking. Back in the sixteenth century at the historic Council of Trent, the Catholic Church rejected the Protestants' insistence on the use of the Bible and the Bible only. And here was their given reason: The church had long before shown authority to reinterpret Scripture—because, influenced by tradition, it transferred the Sabbath to Sunday.

In his book *Canon and Tradition,* Dr. H. J. Holtzmann describes the climactic scene at the Council of Trent. Notice how the decision was reached to give tradition preference in interpreting Scripture:

> Finally . . . on the eighteenth of January, 1562, all hesitation was set aside: the Archbishop of Reggio made a speech in which he openly declared that tradition stood above Scripture. The authority of the Church could therefore not be bound to the authority of the Scriptures, because the Church had changed . . . the Sabbath into Sunday, not by the command of Christ, but by its own authority.

So what carried the day when all hung in the balance? It was the fact that the church had, in effect, changed one of God's commandments, the Sabbath, on the authority of tradition.

Now Protestants may be more surprised than our Catholic friends over this revelation. You see, Roman Catholics have taken pride in what they believe to be the authority of the church in interpreting Scripture. Although I personally cannot accept tradition as having any influence upon belief, I must say that Catholics are at least logical and consistent with their tradition in keeping Sunday.

Perhaps our Protestant friends ought to ask themselves

why they keep Sunday, since obviously tradition figures in its origin. Something to think about, isn't it?

And now one final thought. Were you aware that the Bible provides a special description of God's faithful people just before the coming of Jesus? Let's read it in Revelation 14:12: "Here is the patience of the saints; here are those who keep the commandments of God and the faith of Jesus."

Faith in Jesus and keeping God's commandments—they go together, you see. Evidently in earth's final hour sincere Christians everywhere will be keeping God's commandments. All ten of them.

Whatever our differences may be, we can appreciate each other. And I find so much that I like about my Catholic friends. More than anything else, I admire the dedication of many thousands of Catholics around the world who have given their lives to relieve the suffering of fellow human beings.

I know of no greater reflection of Christ's love than that shown by Maximilian Kolbe, a Polish Franciscan priest who sacrificed his life during the second world war. Imprisoned at the Auschwitz death camp, Kolbe day by day encouraged his fellow sufferers. He shared his meager rations with the sick and weak, even though he was often worse off than those he helped. He led the prisoners in prayer, bringing the light of Christ to that dark death camp.

The SS captors were infuriated by Kolbe's Christianity. They beat him savagely, but he only prayed for them. And finally he paid the ultimate price for his faith and love.

One afternoon the awful sirens began to wail. A prisoner had escaped. In retaliation, ten men were selected to die for their missing companion. One of the doomed ten, a young father, collapsed in broken-hearted sobs, thinking of his family.

Suddenly Kolbe stepped forward. "What do you want?" the death-squad commander snarled.

Kolbe quietly replied, "I want to die in place of this prisoner."

The hardened Nazi was shocked speechless. Finally he found words: "Request granted."

Kolbe was shoved into an underground dungeon and abandoned to starvation. During his last days, as life shriveled away, he was heard praying and singing. Finally the priest breathed his last, faithful unto death. I want to meet that dear saint in heaven.

And I want to be faithful to God's Word, come what may, don't you? God grant us all such faith in Him and love for one another that we can face the challenge of earth's final hours.

Writer Clifford Goldstein earnestly making a point during his visit with George Vandeman as the interview was taped in Washington, D.C., for the "What I Like About Our Jewish Friends" television program.

What I Like About Our Jewish Friends

Israeli guerrillas stirred in their mountain hideout. An army of unsuspecting Syrians swarmed on the plain below. The ambush was set.

So began history's first fight for religious liberty, more than 2,000 years ago. The crisis occurred in 168 B.C. when Antiochus Epiphanes determined to enforce the state religion throughout his kingdom.

Antiochus dispatched patrols in Palestine to promote pagan worship. He built a statue to the idol Jupiter in the Jerusalem temple. Not content with such outrage, he committed the ultimate sacrilege by sacrificing swine on the temple altar. All who refused to forfeit their faith faced death.

Jerusalem seethed with unrest. Things boiled over when Mattathias, an elderly village priest, defied a Syrian officer's command to kneel at the pagan altar. He instead drew his sword and killed his persecutor. Then he fled with his five sons. Although Mattathias died, his sons, led by Judah, promised to keep the faith.

Judah Maccabee assembled an ill-equipped but heroic army of freedom fighters willing to fight to the death for the sake of conscience. Their three-year struggle marked the first successful use of guerrilla tactics—lightning strikes and retreats, ambushes, night raids.

Vastly outnumbered and critically under-armed, their cause seemed doomed. But their leader remained unshaken. "Be brave," he exhorted. "In the sight of heaven it makes no difference to deliver by many or by few."

Courageously the Israelis responded to their leader's challenge. Antiochus rallied his army to crush the revolt, but the Syrians suffered defeat.

Not to be deterred, Antiochus deployed more troops. But the intrepid Israelis overcame them too.

Next came invasion from an even larger force. So sure were the Syrians of victory this time that they brought along slave traders to carry away the vanquished enemy. Judah met this army near the town of Emmaus and put them to flight, capturing weapons and supplies enough to equip 10,000 soldiers.

In the final, decisive battle in 165 B.C., a band of only several thousand Israelis routed an army of 47,000 horsemen, foot soldiers, and spearmen mounted on elephants.

Jerusalem was saved. The joyful victors cleansed the sanctuary and rededicated the temple. Each winter, lovers of liberty around the world celebrate this deliverance in the eight-day festival of Hanukkah.

Were you aware that Christianity's future existence hung in the balance during the Maccabean crisis? The Israeli victory over Antiochus preserved a one-God religious heritage to be carried around the globe by Christianity, Judaism, and Islam.

Now a word about our guest in this chapter. Circumstances somewhat similar to those explained in the last few pages, "What I Like About the Catholics," led me to invite Clifford Goldstein to share with us. Although Jewish by birth, he is now a Christian who has dedicated his life to improving relations between the Jewish and Christian communities. Clifford is an accomplished writer and is also the editor of the magazine *Shabbat Shalom*. We talked together in Washington, D.C., recently.

VANDEMAN: Clifford Goldstein, we're so happy to talk with you today. Could we start by getting acquainted a bit? Where were you born?

GOLDSTEIN: Well, like most American Jews, I was born in New York. Then, as many Jewish people have, I grew up in Miami Beach. And I even lived in Israel for a while. I suppose the big difference is that while living in Israel I became a believer in Jesus as the Messiah.

VANDEMAN: Where in Israel were you living when you accepted Jesus?

GOLDSTEIN: I was in a kibbutz way up in northern Galilee right along the edge of the Golan Heights. I was baptized in the Jordan River. It was really very exciting.

VANDEMAN: It must have been thrilling. Tell us how you relate your Jewish heritage to your Christian faith.

GOLDSTEIN: Well, to me, my Jewish heritage is very inspiring. When you hear about the Jews and the way they have survived all these years, it's like reading an adventure story. The thing I find most thrilling is that we go back so many years. When pagan neighbors around were sacrificing their children to all these various deities, the Jews were ministers and priests in God's beautiful temple. When London and Paris were nothing but swamps, the Jews already had Jerusalem, this beautiful city at the crossroads of the world.

VANDEMAN: A remarkable history indeed. So you

KIBBUTZ — A COLLECTIVE, CHIEFLY AGRA-
CULTURAL COMMUNITY IN ISRAEL.

probably know something about Christianity's indebtedness to the Jewish faith.

GOLDSTEIN: I've come to really understand much about the purpose of Judaism, especially as a believer, and why the Lord raised up the Jews for a unique work. Christians today owe many things to the Jews. Of course, the Bible, both Old and New Testaments, is Jewish from beginning to end. Its concepts are all Jewish. And Jesus, of course, is as Jewish as they come. The idea of one God, the preservation of His law, the whole concept of sacrifice and Messianic redemption—all are truths Christians have received through their Jewish heritage.

VANDEMAN: And what a tremendous heritage it is! Thank you so much for your insights.

No question about it—we Christians owe so much to our Jewish heritage. Think about it. We worship the same God. We treasure the same Hebrew Scriptures. When troubled, we find comfort in the same psalms.

Both Jewish and Christian children delight in the same stories—David and Goliath, Daniel in the lions' den, the brave and beautiful Queen Esther. We honor the same fathers of faith—Abraham, Moses, Elijah, and many more. We even cherish identical values, based upon God's Ten Commandments.

Yes, Jewish and Christian believers share so much in our religion. The major difference between us, of course, is faith in Jesus as the Saviour, or Messiah. But there are divisions even among Jewish scholars about the meaning of Messiah—and other beliefs too.

Within Judaism we find three major branches—the Orthodox, the Reform, and the Conservative. Let's explore each of them briefly.

Orthodox Judaism rigorously abides by two standards—the Torah and the Talmud. The Torah is the five books of Moses, and the Talmud is an explanation or expansion of the Torah authored by ancient rabbis.

The Orthodox strictly observe the scriptural laws of diet and honor the holy days. In worship they preserve Old World practice by not having instrumental music. Men and women sit separately in the synagogues, worshiping with covered heads.

Most Orthodox also believe in a form of religious government in Israel, accompanied by a spiritual revival. They anticipate Jewish people returning to the Holy Land. Some would rebuild the temple and once again offer animal sacrifices. Above all they look forward to the coming of God's Messiah.

Reform Judaism is the liberal wing. They value the Talmud as inspired, but do not bind themselves to all its traditions. So they tend to disregard teachings they feel offer no purpose for the present.

The Reform do not generally believe that a personal Messiah must come amid restored temple worship in Jerusalem. But they still look for an age of messianic peace.

Between the Reform and the Orthodox stand the Conservatives. They treasure the traditions and rituals of the Talmud, as well as the teachings of the Torah—though not quite as strictly as the Orthodox do. And like the Reform, Conservatives are willing to adapt somewhat to modern society.

Which is the largest branch of Judaism in the United States? The Orthodox have by far the most synagogues. But most American Jewish people identify themselves as Conservative or Reform. Various subgroups also flourish, a major one being the Reconstructionist movement.

Even though congregations have full independence, they manage to maintain an extraordinary unity. This is especially remarkable, since Jewish people have been scattered from their homeland for the last 2,000 years.

Long ago, the teenage exiles Joseph and Daniel brought blessing to the land of their captivity. Jewish immigrants have always enriched their host country in manifold ways. Many of history's finest and most famous—musicians, scientists, lawyers, artisans, entertainers, business people, generals, philosophers, and statesmen—have been Jewish. Unquestionably the United States would not be the great nation she is today were it not for the contribution of our Jewish people.

Early in colonial history, Jewish refugees sought freedom in our land of liberty. Yet even here they suffered prejudice and some persecution. But not always.

For example, Jewish settlers from Portugal found safety in Dutch New Amsterdam. In 1654 they established the first official synagogue in the New World. By 1850, seventy-seven Jewish congregations had organized in twenty-one states. Today 3,500 synagogues in North America serve our seven million Jewish people.

Jewish people still suffer prejudice and discrimination—and much of it comes from supposed Christians. We are painfully aware that Adolph Hitler rose to power and massacred millions of Jewish people in a land of rich Christian heritage.

Of course, Hitler did not practice Christianity. And German believers were shocked by the unspeakable horrors of his death camps. But we cannot deny that Hitler tapped into the prejudices and fears many Protestants had for Jewish people.

We Christians sometimes forget that Jesus Himself was Jewish. He was born in the royal bloodline of David from the tribe of Judah. And all His apostles were Jewish.

So why did Jesus' own people reject Him?

For one thing, His claim to be divine seemed out of line.

When He proclaimed, "I and My Father are one," (John 10:30) Jesus seemed to violate a basic principle of Jewish belief. Every devout Hebrew daily repeats the Shema from Deuteronomy 6:4-9: "Hear, O Israel: The Lord our God, the Lord is one!"

Since God is one, how could Jesus dare to share divinity with the Father? This perplexity led the religious leaders of that day to charge Jesus with blasphemy and decide to put Him to death. You can read about it in John 10:30-33.

It would have been helpful to remember the first chapter of the Torah. God had said, "Let *Us* make man in *Our* image, according to *Our* likeness." Genesis 1:26, emphasis supplied.

This plural form for God obviously requires the presence of at least two persons. Yet the plurality of God does not deny His oneness, as we notice in the very next verse: "God created man in His own image." Genesis 1:27.

Evidently there must be one God—a singular God-head—with plural members. Our limited human minds cannot comprehend this, just as we cannot understand how God had no beginning but has existed from eternity.

Yes, these things and many others are impossible to explain. But when we accept the Scriptures as they read, how could we deny them?

At the birth of Jesus, wise men from the East asked where Messiah would be born. King Herod referred them to the priests. And the Jewish leaders pointed toward the little town of Bethlehem, quoting the prophet Micah:

"But you, Bethlehem Ephrathah, though you are little among the thousands of Judah, yet out of you shall come forth to Me the One to be ruler in Israel, whose goings forth have been from of old, from everlasting." Micah 5:2 (verse 1 in Jewish versions).

Apparently the religious leaders of that day missed the last part of the text, which documents the everlasting his-

tory of Messiah. They knew where He would come *to*—
Bethlehem—but they overlooked where He would come
from—eternity.

Other factors contributed to the rejection of Jesus by the
leaders of that day. As in the time of Antiochus, the nation
again suffered the yoke of a foreign government—but this
time with one important difference. Israel enjoyed freedom of religion under the Romans. So the situation was
more of a political inconvenience than a spiritual crisis.

Even so, the nation longed to break away from Rome.
They wanted a Messiah who, like Judah Maccabee, would
drive out the enemy and restore their independence. But
Jesus had no interest in raising armies to save the people
from Romans—He had come to save them from sin.

Since Jesus failed their expectations, Israel failed to accept Him. But the day He hung on the cross, some had
second thoughts.

Imagine a conversation at Calvary between two members of the Jewish high court—Nicodemus and Joseph.
Both have been deeply moved by the teachings of Jesus.
Although neither has yet identified with Him, Joseph se-
cretly believes. Nicodemus, however, still struggles with
doubt.

While the crowd gazes at Jesus in His dying agony, the
two Jewish leaders step aside for a quiet talk. Nicodemus
suggests that if Jesus were indeed Messiah, He would save
Himself from the cross and rescue the nation from Rome.

Joseph points to a passage from the prophet Isaiah:

"He is despised and rejected by men, a man of sorrows
and acquainted with grief. And we hid, as it were, our
faces from Him. . . . He was wounded for our transgressions, He was bruised for our iniquities; the chastisement
for our peace was upon Him, and by His stripes we are
healed. All we like sheep have gone astray; we have
turned, every one, to his own way; and the Lord has laid on

Him the iniquity of us all. . . . He was cut off from the land of the living; for the transgressions of My people He was stricken." Isaiah 53:3-8.

"But how do we know Isaiah was thinking about Messiah here?" Nicodemus wonders."He might have been portraying the persecution of Jewish people—how our nation would suffer from its enemies."

"Look closely at the text," Joseph persists. "It draws a distinction between the Suffering One and our nation: 'We—our nation—hid our faces from Him. He was wounded for our transgressions.'"

Nicodemus is impressed but still perplexed. "Suppose then Isaiah is testifying here of his personal sufferings."

"That couldn't be," Joseph replies. "This passage involves substitutionary punishment from God. It says the suffering One would be 'smitten by God.' 'The Lord has laid on Him the iniquity of us all.' You see, Messiah would bear the curse of sin for our salvation. He's God's sacrificial lamb."

Joseph continues. "Long ago in the wilderness our people were plagued by poisonous snakes. Thousands were dying without hope. God told Moses to form a brass serpent and put it high on a pole for the victims to see. All who looked in faith and believed God would heal them lived. Well, you know the story. In fact, didn't Jesus Himself mention it that night you spoke with Him?"

"Yes, He did," replies Nicodemus. "He told me that just as Moses lifted up the serpent in the wilderness, He must also be lifted up on the cross. As the serpent had been cursed, so He would bear the curse of God. And all who believe in Him would not perish but have eternal life."

As he speaks, Nicodemus lights up with new conviction. "You know, Joseph, I've often thought about what Jesus told me that night. And I can see it all so very clearly now. Messiah is bearing the curse of God on the cross so I can be forgiven. I must look to Him and live."

"But tell me, Joseph. You believe in Jesus. Why have you kept your faith a secret?"

"Up to this point I've been afraid," Joseph admits. "But not anymore. If Jesus can sacrifice His life for me, then I can dedicate my life to Him."

"I will too," says Nicodemus. And together they declare their faith in the Lord Jesus Christ. While they reverently remove His broken body from the cross, the crowd watches quietly.

Many walked home that afternoon deep in thought. And there was much to think about. The confession of the Roman officer: "Truly this Man was the Son of God!" Mark 15:39. The cry of the dying thief: "Lord, remember me when You come into Your kingdom." Luke 23:42. And the prayer of Jesus: "Father, forgive them, for they do not know what they do." Luke 23:34.

Had the crowd been too hasty in condemning Jesus? What if He was Messiah after all?

That night, by the light of Sabbath candles, many probed the prophecies as never before. They learned that David a thousand years before had penned the piercing cry of Jesus: "My God, My God, why have You forsaken Me?" Psalm 22:1.

In the same psalm David foretold the crucifying nails: "They pierced My hands and My feet." Psalm 22:16.

And there was more to discover about Jesus. The soldiers had divided His clothing among themselves. But when they came to His robe, they cast lots for it rather than tear the singly woven piece. This too had been foretold. See Psalm 22:18.

Other prophecies had been fulfilled too. His betrayer sold Jesus for thirty pieces of silver. The money provided a burial place called the "potter's field." All this had been predicted 500 years before. See Zechariah 11:12, 13.

Every prophecy tried on Jesus fit perfectly. Many concluded that Jesus was indeed who He claimed to be—their Messiah.

The most convincing evidence about Jesus is the silent testimony of time. Three and a half years before His death, when beginning His ministry, He had announced, "The time is fulfilled." Mark 1:15.

What time was He talking about? Was there some kind of prophetic countdown involved here?

Indeed there was. Long ago the prophet Daniel predicted: "Know therefore and understand, that from the going forth of the command to restore and build Jerusalem until Messiah the Prince, there shall be seven weeks and sixty-two weeks." Daniel 9:25.

In Daniel's time, you recall, Jerusalem lay in ruins. But God in His mercy promised to restore the city. The command by King Artaxerxes went forth in 457 B.C. You can read about it in the Bible book of Ezra, chapter 7.

From 457 B.C. until Messiah appeared, there would be "seven weeks and sixty-two weeks." That's 69 weeks, or 483 prophetic years (7 times 69 = 483). In A.D. 27—exactly 483 years after the commandment to restore Jerusalem, Christ was baptized and began His mission as Messiah.

There's more to Daniel's prophecy. In the "middle of the week"—three and a half years later—Messiah was to be "cut off," that is, put to death. See Daniel 9:26, 27. And it happened right on schedule!

Is it any wonder that, down through the centuries, thousands of Jewish people have considered Jesus to be the fulfillment of their heritage? A glorious heritage we all share together.

During the darkest days of World War II, Nazi troops swarmed over Holland, searching for Jewish people. Not many Christians seemed to care. But some did. In the city of Haarlem, Corrie ten Boom opened her heart and home to the ones Hitler hated most.

One afternoon the dreaded Gestapo arrived. As soldiers burst inside, Corrie's family hurried their Jewish friends up the stairs to a secret third-floor room.

The guests escaped, but their hosts did not. At the Ravensbrück concentration camp, Corrie's beloved sister Betsie died. Corrie herself was scheduled for the gas chamber, but a clerical "mistake" set her free.

Did Corrie succumb to bitterness from her suffering and loss? No, friend. And she never regretted her sacrifice in saving Jewish refugees. You see, they were her brothers and sisters.

Yes, whether Christians or Jewish, we are all God's family together. May God help us appreciate each other as we seek to follow His will.

Why So Many Denominations?

Have you ever asked yourself this question? Probably so. And the answer is not difficult to find—especially in the wake of the information found in the preceding pages of this book.

At this point we pause in our examination of individual churches to discover a prophecy in the heart of the Revelation which should give us all courage. It will show that God understands our dilemma and longs to give meaning to the confusion some people feel when confronted with so many "roads to heaven." This is one enigma I have always felt someone should address. So here it is.

Let me begin by taking you on a fascinating journey to the Alps of northern Italy—a panorama of breathtaking beauty. Here we find snowcapped peaks in their towering majesty. Rich green valleys watered by clear-running streams. Rolling meadows carpeted with wildflowers. Hillside orchards ripening with luscious fruit.

This is God's country, almost heaven on earth. But something tragic happened here many years ago. The snow became red with blood—the blood of God's people.

Some heartbreaking yet faith-inspiring history awaits you in this chapter. And a fascinating Bible prophecy too.

Hundreds of years ago, there lived in the Italian Alps a gentle people called the Waldenses. Their faith was fresh

ALSO EPHESIANS 4:15-16 ALL CHURCHS FIT TOGETHER
LIVING BIBLE   LIKE A PUZZLE

as the crisp mountain air, enduring as the evergreens, pure as the virgin snow. For a thousand years they kept the lamp of truth shining amid spiritual darkness. The Waldenses preserved the ancient faith once delivered to the saints by Jesus Himself and the apostles. Faith which had suffered centuries of neglect and abuse by the religious establishment.

We will meet the Waldenses again later in this chapter. But first let me ask you something. Should the erosion of faith by the Christian church surprise us? After all, the Old Testament records an ongoing affair with apostasy. And the New Testament predicted history would repeat itself. Once again a falling away from truth would corrupt true faith, the apostles Peter and Paul both warned. See 2 Peter 2:1, 2; Acts 20:29, 30.

The book of Revelation also foretold the struggles of God's people during the Christian era. Would you come with me to chapter 12? Let's read verses 1 and 2: "Now a great sign appeared in heaven: a woman clothed with the sun, with the moon under her feet, and on her head a garland of twelve stars. Then being with child, she cried out in labor and in pain to give birth." Revelation 12:1, 2.

Who is this woman? In the Bible God often uses the symbol of a woman to represent a church—a pure woman to represent His sincere followers, and an immoral woman to represent fallen Christianity. See 2 Corinthians 11:2; Ephesians 5:21-23. So this pure woman of Revelation 12 must represent God's faithful people. And notice that the woman was with child. A child under attack.

Look at verses 3 and 4: "Another sign appeared in heaven: behold, a great, fiery red dragon. . . . And the dragon stood before the woman who was ready to give birth, to devour her Child as soon as it was born." Revelation 12:3, 4.

The dragon here is none other than Satan, mortal enemy of the church. Remember how the devil, working through Herod, the Roman ruler, tried to destroy Christ by murdering all male babies in Bethlehem? But infant Jesus escaped with His mother Mary and Joseph. You know the story.

After Christ grew up and began His ministry, the enemy attacked Him with a new strategy. He approached the Lord in the wilderness with several shrewd temptations. But Jesus refused to compromise His faith.

Enraged, Satan tried yet another tactic. He entrapped the religious leaders with his deceptions. Once he gained control of the religious establishment of that time, the enemy employed the leaders in persecuting Jesus. They apparently conquered Christ at the cross, but He rose victorious from the grave to ascend to the throne of God. Notice verse 5: "She [the church] bore a male Child who was to rule all nations with a rod of iron. And her Child was caught up to God and to His throne." Revelation 12:5.

The devil was thoroughly frustrated in his attacks upon the Son of God. So now he turned upon the woman—the church. He attacked God's people with the identical strategy he had tried against Jesus. History repeated itself in a remarkable way. Listen to what happened.

First the devil tried to kill the infant church. He used Roman rulers as his agents, just as he had with Baby Jesus. But despite fierce persecution by Nero and his successors, Christianity survived and thrived. Satan realized he could not destroy God's people by violence.

So the enemy approached the church with subtle temptations. He determined to lure its leaders into compromising their faith. Many refused to yield, remaining faithful as their Lord had been when He was tempted. But the enemy did manage once again to manipulate the religious establishment of that day. As in the time of Christ, truth became buried under tradition.

God's faithful people, refusing to participate in apostasy, were marked for death, as their Lord had been. History records the tragic story. Religious leaders martyred millions of sincere believers for no greater crime than faithfully following the Word of God. For many dark centuries, the saints had to go into hiding. We see in verse 6: "Then the woman fled into the wilderness, where she had a place prepared by God, that they should feed her there one thousand two hundred and sixty days." Revelation 12:6.

Here we have a time prophecy—a period of persecution lasting 1,260 days. Are these days literal or symbolic? It is helpful to recall that the book of Revelation deals in symbols. Remember too that the persecution lasted many centuries—much longer than 1,260 actual days. It was more like 1,260 years. Is this the time frame indicated by the prophecy—1,260 years?

Apparently, in symbolic prophecy a day must represent a year. See Ezekiel 4:6. This is what the reformers taught. Martin Luther and others believed that this time period represented 1,260 years of oppression by the church of the Middle Ages.

And history confirms it. In the sixth century, the church influenced Emperor Justinian to issue a decree withdrawing all protection from the heretics, as God's faithful ones were called. And that persecution had reached its unbridled fury by A.D. 538. Adding 1,260 years to 538 would bring us down to a little before our time—1798. In that very year Napoleon interrupted the power which had oppressed the faithful.

So during the dark centuries, as the prophecy of Revelation 12 foretold, God's people went into hiding. Verse 16 tells us that "the earth helped the woman." The mountains of the Alps and other remote places of the earth provided the church protection, and she survived. Through it all the light of truth never went out completely, though it burned quite dim.

The Waldenses! Come with me to visit their secret chapel, called *Chiesa de la Tanna,* which means "Church of the Earth." On hands and knees you can make your way down the rocky tunnel to their underground meeting room. In this cave, perfectly camouflaged by nature, the Waldenses for many years worshiped undetected.

But at last came the day when scores of them were trapped here by soldiers who built a fire in its opening. As the oxygen was consumed, the Waldenses sang praises to God until breath was gone, glad to give their lives rather than renounce their faith.

No one knows how many true believers spilled their blood during the long exile of the church in the wilderness. But just as God watched over His Son, so He preserved His people. As Jesus came forth from the grave victorious, the church finally emerged from its wilderness hibernation.

At this point I should mention that the word *church* here does not mean denomination—the Lutheran denomination, the Baptist denomination, the Adventist denomination—No. In the New Testament, the word *church* from the Greek word *ekklesia,* simply means God's "called-out ones." Don't you like that? Would you want to be one of God's called-out ones?

Let's consider an illustration that helps us understand the experience of God's people in Revelation 12. Suppose, if you will, that you are standing on a hillside overlooking a giant plain stretching for miles into the distance. You notice that a railroad track—a single track—crosses the plain and disappears into a tunnel.

Suddenly you hear the sound of a train approaching. And then you see it—a grand old Baldwin locomotive with two familiar passenger cars. It speeds along at seventy miles an hour, shall we say. On a single track, remember.

Now if a black locomotive with its fine Pullman cars disappears into one end of the tunnel, wouldn't you expect the same black locomotive with the same Pullman cars to emerge from the other end? Of course you would.

But what if a black locomotive with two Pullman cars goes into one side of the mountain, and out the other side comes a modern diesel locomotive pulling several sight-seeing passenger cars? You would say, "Something must have happened to the train inside the tunnel." And of course, you would be right.

Now, please forget these trains for a moment. And let's imagine that the true church started down the track of time at the beginning of the Christian era. Picture the church of Revelation 12 in its pure faith riding down through the centuries—past the first century, past the second century, the third, and the fourth. By the year 538 it becomes necessary, in order to preserve its faith, to go into hiding. So it disappears into the wilderness tunnel for more than a thousand years.

Let me ask you this. Wouldn't we expect the same church—teaching the same body of truth—which disappeared from sight so many years earlier, to emerge from the wilderness tunnel teaching the same message the early Christians taught? We certainly would.

But what if out of the tunnel comes not one church but many churches, many different denominations? You would say something must have happened in the wilderness tunnel! And of course, you would be right!

Church history reveals that something disturbing did happen during the Middle Ages. Truth suffered. It became fragmented—yet it survived. We have noticed how God intervened to restore neglected truth—how He raised Reformers to bring back truth which had been forgotten during the long centuries in the wilderness.

Martin Luther appeared on the scene to restore the heartbeat of Christianity. And the Reformation began— but it was not finished in the sixteenth century. Light had only begun to break forth in the wilderness tunnel.

Really now, could we expect that all of the truths hidden for so long would be recovered immediately—all at once? No, not likely. Luther rediscovered that forgiveness comes by faith alone in Jesus Christ. So we have our Lutheran Church. But the importance of certain other truths was not seen clearly by Luther. Some of these neglected truths we have already discussed in this book, such as adult baptism, which was recovered by the Anabaptists.

Anabaptists approached the leading Protestant scholars and urged them to accept this new light. We might have hoped they would, but they didn't. So we have our Baptist Church today. And when other truths came through Wesley, the established churches turned him down. That gave birth to the Methodists. The story goes on and on.

Do you see our problem? It's the sad human tendency to depend upon the past, to draw a circle about our beliefs and call it a creed. These original creeds helped restate the foundation of Christianity. But they did not make provision for advancing light. So we have our many denominations today.

Remember again what God had said in Proverbs 4:18: "The path of the just is as the shining light, that shineth more and more unto the perfect day." Truth, if we follow it, will shine brighter and brighter. Ever more glorious. Always advancing. Never retreating. Never standing still.

Can we see what God is attempting to do? He wants to preserve every ray of light each Reformer so carefully guarded, adding to them newly discovered truth which also had been lost through the centuries. Would He not want to present this total package—this message in its original beauty—to a world so desperately in need?

And it has been happening. Slowly but surely, truths long hidden have been emerging from the confusion of the dark centuries. As additional truths are recovered, other movements have sprung into existence, each championing newly rediscovered light.

Let's look at the last verse of Revelation 12: "The dragon [Satan] was enraged with the woman [the church], and he went to make war with the rest of her offspring, who keep the commandments of God and have the testimony of Jesus Christ." Revelation 12:17.

Here we have a description of God's last-day people. (Remember, we are not talking about denominations in particular now, rather simply God's people.) Did you notice their twin identifying marks? Keeping the commandments of God and holding to the testimony of Jesus. Faith in Christ and keeping God's commandments go together.

The Ten Commandments—could they contain neglected truth? Perhaps as a child you memorized them. What about the fourth commandment? Is this not a very neglected truth? Did you ever notice that the fourth commandment, the Sabbath commandment, is different from the others? Nine of the commandments tell us what we must do for God and neighbor. But the Sabbath commandment tells us what God has done for us. And it invites us to share in the rest God earned by His work.

Let's read that fourth commandment together: "Remember the Sabbath day, to keep it holy. Six days you shall labor and do all your work, but the seventh day is the Sabbath of the Lord your God. In it you shall do no work. . . . For in six days the Lord made the heavens and the earth . . . and rested the seventh day. Therefore the Lord blessed the Sabbath day and hallowed it." Exodus 20:8-11.

The seventh-day Sabbath, you see, invites us to celebrate God's work for us as our Creator. And there's another reason why we worship God. There's another reason to keep the seventh day holy.

Come with me reverently to Calvary. It's late Friday afternoon, nearly time to welcome the Sabbath. Jesus, hanging on the cross, recalls all He has done for our salvation. Then with His dying breath He proclaims, "It is finished!" Mission accomplished! Mankind redeemed.

Again Jesus rests on the Sabbath in honor of His finished work, just as He did after creation. Only this time He rests in the tomb. Following Sabbath rest Christ arises and ascends to heaven's throne.

Now, the idea of worshiping on Saturday, the seventh-day Sabbath of the fourth commandment, may be new to you. Or you may have heard that Sabbath keeping is legalistic. Well, nothing could be further from the truth. You see, the word *sabbath* itself means "rest." That's the *opposite* of works. Each week the Sabbath points us away from human works to rest in God's work for us. And that, my friend, is the gospel! Without Sabbath rest, you see, our obedience to God's law would be legalism.

Never forget it—we are not saved by keeping the law. We are saved by resting in Christ. That, I say, is the gospel. And that is also the message of the Sabbath. Amid the essential duties outlined in the law, the Sabbath offers us rest in the work of Christ for us.

Now we understand why Jesus proclaimed Himself "Lord of the Sabbath." We show our faith in Jesus, our Maker and Redeemer, by resting on the seventh day. The Sabbath memorializes the greatest things our Lord has done for us—the reasons we worship Him.

This brings us to a question. Since the seventh day, which we call Saturday, is evidently God's day of worship, how is it that most Christians keep the first day of the week, Sunday? We saw in an earlier chapter that the church of the Middle Ages, without authorization from Scripture, took responsibility for changing the Sabbath to

Sunday. As late as the sixteenth century, faithful Christians here and there still kept the seventh day holy. A number of Anabaptists, for example, observed the Sabbath, despite fierce persecution.

Finally the neglected, nearly forgotten truth about the seventh-day Sabbath was recovered. And since the nineteenth century, millions of Christians around the world have begun worshiping on the Bible Sabbath.

What a heritage God has for us today, highlighting truths recaptured by the Reformers—and now in the final moments of the Reformation, still rediscovering truth. Shouldn't we all keep following advancing light? What a challenge for the alert, thinking Christian!

And now as we near the close of this chapter, may I share with you a delightful little story I came across not long ago? A boy was herding sheep for his father. And not far away, across a valley, a neighbor lad was herding his father's sheep. The boys were good friends.

One day a severe storm came up very suddenly, and the boys, with their sheep, took refuge. When the storm was over and it was time to go home, the boys had a problem. They couldn't separate the sheep. Some of them they knew. But they weren't sure about others.

Finally, in desperation, and fearful that they would be scolded, they started for home—one down one path and one down another. And what do you think happened? The sheep just separated themselves perfectly, each sheep following his own shepherd!

Do you see? You could take any sheep in those flocks and tell whom it belonged to—by which shepherd it followed. That's the way to tell!

Are you one of Christ's sheep? You are if you follow Him as He reveals His truth in His Word, whatever that truth may be. And you can make that decision before the Lord just now.

President Neal Wilson, world leader of the Seventh-day Adventist Church, shares a conviction with George Vandeman during the television taping session of his testimony.

What I Like About the Adventists

He was an American patriot, a captain in the War of 1812. He was also a confirmed skeptic who ridiculed religion. But then he experienced a dramatic conversion and became a Baptist minister. Many thousands from all denominations flocked to hear him preach.

His name? William Miller, an American Reformer. One of the most fascinating characters of the early nineteenth century.

William Miller might have been the last one you would expect to lead a religious awakening. To him, faith in Jesus meant mere superstition. A rugged individualist from sturdy New England stock, Miller believed that decent, law-and-order patriotism was the salvation of society.

When America's newly won independence was challenged by the British in the War of 1812, Miller volunteered for military service. Forty-seven of his neighbors also joined, on condition that they be placed directly under Miller's command.

After distinguishing himself in the decisive battle of Plattsburg, Miller returned to the family farm in upstate New York. Now and then he attended the local Baptist church, only out of politeness to his mother. But before long he became concerned about his spiritual condition.

97

Convicted by the Holy Spirit, he wrestled in despair over his sins. How wonderful it would be to throw himself into the arms of a Saviour and be forgiven!

But how could he know Jesus Christ even existed? Miller set aside his prejudice and opened the Bible. There in its pages, he met the living Lord. As he testified later, "I was constrained to admit that the Scriptures must be a revelation from God. They became my delight, and in Jesus I found a friend."

Immediately his skeptic friends taunted Miller, just as he had mercilessly taunted other Christians. They scoffed, "How do you know the Bible is the Word of God? What about its contradictions?"

Miller countered, "If the Bible is the Word of God, all its parts can be made to harmonize. Give me time, and I'll prove it."

Laying aside every book but the Bible itself and a concordance, Miller began his study with the first verse of Genesis 1. He advanced no more quickly than he could handle questions that confronted him. Miller used one text to unlock the meaning of another, permitting the Bible to explain itself. One by one, its seeming inconsistencies faded away.

Best of all, Miller learned that Jesus, his Friend and Saviour, had promised to return to earth. The conviction fastened upon him that he had a responsibility to spread the good news about the approaching advent, or coming of Christ. But he wasn't a preacher. Yet his conscience kept prodding him, "Go and tell the world."

For thirteen years Miller resisted the call. Finally one morning in 1831, he promised the Lord he would preach about the second coming—but only if he received an invitation. Within the hour a messenger arrived with a request from the Baptist church in nearby Dresden. They wanted to hear about the second advent of Jesus.

Miller was terrified. But how could he reject so definite a call? Right from the start it was obvious that this humble man enjoyed the blessing of heaven. Seventy converts to Christ were reaped from his first preaching series. In one place a hundred infidels accepted his message in a single week.

Before long, Miller's sound Bible preaching brought him many more speaking invitations than he could accept. Churches of various denominations vied with one another to draw him away from his farm and into their pulpits. As the demand for his preaching skyrocketed, Miller left his farm and entered the full-time ministry. By this time he had received a Baptist minister's license. And forty-three pastors from various denominations signed a certificate of "Ministerial Recommendation" on his behalf.

At this point a number of clergy left their salaries to join the advent movement—Methodist ministers, Baptists, Congregationalists, Lutherans, Episcopalians, Dutch Reformed—to name just a few. These educated students of the Word provided creative contributions of their own to Miller's message. Before long, shock waves rippled through the nation as many thousands crowded huge tents and meeting halls to hear the startling news of Christ's soon return.

The Adventist movement in North America was part of a worldwide awakening of interest in Christ's second coming. In England, several hundred ministers preached the soon return of Jesus. The advent message was also presented in South America and Germany. And in Sweden and Norway, young people—even children too young to read or write—explained with earnestness and power the prophecies of a soon-coming Saviour.

One of the chief heralds of the advent was Joseph Wolff, known as "missionary to the world." From his study of Bible prophecy, he expected Christ to return in the year

1847. For eighteen years he traveled and preached in Africa, Asia, the Middle East, India, and North America. He even proclaimed the soon return of Jesus, upon invitation, before the assembled Congress of the United States.

The advent message startled Christianity out of its slumber. You see, the news of Christ's second coming had become a neglected truth. Back in the days of the apostles, it was the burning obsession of the early Christians. In fact, the apostle Paul proclaimed Christ's return to be their "blessed hope." But as the centuries passed, the second advent of Jesus seemed nearly forgotten. It joined the list of neglected truths we have discussed in this book.

But God was not content to leave His light buried under a bushel of medieval darkness. So in the sixteenth century He called the Reformers on the scene to champion truth that had been overlooked through the years. Then God's people emerged completely from their centuries in the wilderness—right on schedule, according to the prophecy of Revelation 12. Now it was time to revive yet another first-century teaching of the apostles. William Miller and the Adventists were called to restore the blessed hope of Christ's soon return.

The world was ripe for the advent message. Caught up with the dawning Industrial Revolution, society had turned away from religion to trust in human accomplishment. Churches of the day generally taught that conditions on earth would improve and usher in a golden age of peace. It should not surprise us, then, that many resisted the news that Christ would come soon and interrupt the good life on planet Earth.

Some who believed in the soon coming of Christ were disfellowshiped by their churches. Others withdrew on their own to join with fellow Adventists who were looking for the Lord's immediate return.

William Miller and his followers expected Christ to

come in 1844. When that time passed without the appearance of Jesus, disappointment crushed the believers. You can imagine how they felt. Many lost heart and gave up the faith. Others, convinced that God was with them, continued their study of the Bible.

Soon they were reminded of something that brought immense comfort and relief. Long ago there had also been a religious movement which had suffered a great disappointment—the Christian church itself. When Jesus died on the cross, His disciples felt crushed, confused, and utterly defeated. With the scoffing of unbelievers ringing in their ears, they mourned, "We were hoping that it was He who was going to redeem Israel." Luke 24:21.

Yet even though the disciples' expectations had failed, God was still with them. He had been leading them all along and planned a bright future for their movement.

Likewise, the Adventists had been led by God during their great disappointment. Although many became discouraged and forfeited the blessed hope, others became more convinced than ever that God had been leading them and had plans for their future.

Before long, additional light came to an Adventist group in New England through a young Seventh Day Baptist woman. She called their attention to the fourth commandment, showing that God had never withdrawn Sabbath rest from His people. True, the Sabbath had been nearly forgotten during the dark centuries. Yet the seventh day remains an eternal memorial of the work of Jesus. Adventists eagerly accepted this unexpected gem of neglected truth.

By the way, have you ever studied how denominations chose their names? Some churches are named according to the structure that governs them. Episcopalian, for example, means that bishops have supreme authority in the church. And Congregational shows that local congregations make decisions for themselves.

Another group of churches are named after their founders. Outstanding among these is the Lutherans, in honor of Martin Luther.

Then you have churches that take their names from important truths they teach. Right away I think of the Baptists, named after their belief in the New Testament form of baptism. Of course, all who are baptized by immersion are Baptists in the general sense. And those who belong to that body of believers are Baptists in the specific sense.

Now tell me, do you believe in the second advent of Jesus? Then you can consider yourself an Adventist, in a general sense. Seventh-day Adventists take their name from two basic truths about Jesus which they hold dear. "Adventist," of course, refers to their belief that Jesus is coming soon. "Seventh-day" lets people know they observe the day which honors Christ as Creator and Redeemer. So the name *Seventh-day Adventist* proclaims truth about Jesus, neglected truth, that needed to be recovered to complete the Reformation.

It has been my privilege in this book to share a number of neglected truths recovered by the Lutherans, Methodists, Baptists, and other groups. But remember, the Reformation was not finished long ago when the earliest Reformers died. Started, yes—but not completed. And the Bible tells us that additional neglected truth would shine forth in the last days.

And that shouldn't surprise us, should it? Remember Proverbs 4:18: "The path of the just is as the shining light, that shineth more and more unto the perfect day."

Light will continue to shine, you see, until that perfect day when Jesus comes. And whatever additional light God graciously shows us in His Word should be welcomed, wouldn't you say?

I think you can begin to see why I have chosen as my

spiritual home the Seventh-day Adventist family. More and more Christians have come to share my convictions. Did you know that Seventh-day Adventists are among the three fastest-growing churches in the world today? More than a thousand people every day—that's more than 365,000 each year—are joining this body of believers. Adventist world membership now totals five million.

There are good reasons why so many earnest Christians are looking toward the Adventists. They believe this group has gathered together gems of light, the truths championed through the years by all denominations—the neglected truths of the centuries. First of all, the faith in Christ of the Lutherans. And then the baptism by immersion of the Baptists. The interest in Christian growth and Spirit-filled living of the Methodists and Charismatics. The respect for morality of the Catholics. The Sabbath championed by our Jewish ancestors and cherished by Jesus and the apostles. All of these truths, you see, Adventists united into one body of belief.

And as Adventists continued to study the Bible, further truth unfolded. They came to realize that the human body is the temple of the Holy Spirit. See 1 Corinthians 6:19. Therefore good religion takes an interest in good health. What affects the body affects the mind and spirit too. So Adventists lay aside tobacco and liquor and emphasize the advantages of exercise, fresh air, sunshine, a balanced diet, adequate rest, and trust in God.

Does it pay? It certainly does. The nonalcoholic, nonsmoking Adventist lifestyle, with its appetizing natural-food diet, helps its members live six to seven years longer than the general population, according to recent surveys—with only half the cancer and heart disease.

And Adventists have lived that way for well over a century, long before nutrition achieved the status of a full-fledged science. Where did they get their inside information? In part, from an extraordinary woman named Ellen White.

Ellen White warned of the poisons in tobacco when doctors of her day hailed smoking as a cure for lung problems. In 1868 she cautioned about the effects of animal fat upon the bloodstream. And that was long before the words *cholesterol* and *polyunsaturated* found their way into dictionaries. She recommended a diet of whole grains with plenty of fruits and vegetables. Today we know full well about the benefits of fiber. She advised against the overuse of refined foods, particularly flour and sugar, long before scientists even suspected there were such things as vitamins which could be destroyed in the refining process.

Ellen White's books still ride the crest of discoveries in medical research, more than seventy years after her death. And everything she taught about health is rooted in the New Testament principle that our bodies are the temples of the Holy Spirit.

Let me tell you more about this remarkable woman, Ellen White. She authored more than fifty books spanning a range of topics from child training to practical Christianity, from scholastics to nutrition and health. Her best seller, *Steps to Christ,* has been translated into 125 languages—more than any other book ever authored by a woman. Yet, hampered by a childhood accident, she never made it past the third grade.

How did Ellen White get such inside information without an education? She had no medical training whatsoever. Of course, she was well-read, frequently using the language of other authors to get her point across. But she had amazing discernment to select the best and reject the rest.

How did she know what to take and what to leave? Adventists believe she received a special gift from God to bring counsel and encouragement to His people.

Despite her remarkable revelations, Ellen White remained humble. She insisted that the Bible always remain the only foundation of Christian teaching. When some enthusiastic members would seem to value her books on a par with Scripture, she kindly but firmly set them straight.

Ellen White was a loving and lovable Christian who touched thousands of lives with her sincerity, sympathy, and generosity. But please don't take my word about her inside information. Examine her books for yourself. See if your heart isn't warmed. See if your soul isn't inspired to draw closer to your Saviour.

And now I'd like to take you to Washington, D.C. Let's visit the world headquarters of the Seventh-day Adventist Church and meet its president, Pastor Neal C. Wilson.

VANDEMAN: Pastor Wilson, I'm so pleased that my own president can be with us today. Welcome!

WILSON: It's a joy to be with you, George. And I think you know how much I appreciate the unique television ministry of "It Is Written."

VANDEMAN: That's kind of you, Neal, thank you. Tell me, why are you a *Christian?*

WILSON: My father and mother were wonderful examples of practical Christianity. But I grew up and was educated on several different continents and so was exposed to a wide spectrum of Christian belief, as well as to many Eastern religions. In this setting I had opportunity as a young man to discuss and read widely. Ultimately, I had to decide whether I could really accept Christianity for myself or whether I was going to follow some other religion.

Everywhere I saw the tragic results of sin. I also sensed personally the reason why the apostle said, "The good that I would I do not: but the evil that I would not, that I do." And I understood from experience his statement in Romans where he said, "O wretched man that I am! who shall deliver me from this body of death? [Romans 7:19, 21, KJV]."

Many times I heard it said that it was through good works—my works—that atonement could be made. But then I discovered that the Christian way is a different way. It is based on Christ's works, not mine—His atonement, His life, His intercession. He came to be the center of my life and my belief. He offers salvation freely to me through faith alone by His grace. And that's everything.

When I discovered that, I gave my life in total abandonment to Christ—my Friend, my Saviour, my Lord. In that assurance, I rejoice today.

VANDEMAN: Thank God. Now, why are you a *Seventh-day Adventist* Christian, Neal?

WILSON: Well, that goes a step further. The closer I came to my Lord and Saviour, Jesus Christ, and the more I studied the Bible, the more I realized that Christianity is more than just a system of beliefs. It is a love relationship with Jesus Christ. And Jesus says, "If you love Me, keep My commandments." [John 14:15.] I began to see that being a Seventh-day Adventist Christian fulfilled that calling for me.

Three points attracted me: first, Seventh-day Adventists have a distinctive body of doctrinal truth. Second, Adventists have a unique feature in their lifestyle—they treat their bodies as the temple of the Holy Spirit. Third, Adventists have a distinctive world view, based on Christ's commission to preach in all the world. For these reasons I've felt compelled to become a Seventh-day Adventist Christian.

VANDEMAN: Beautifully said. Thank you for coming today, Neal.

Just now as we near the close of these pages, I invite you to rejoice with me that Jesus is coming again—one of the urgent neglected truths recovered for our day. Could there be any better news—any better comfort?

I think back to the time of World War II. Those dark days that began with the blitzkrieg of Poland. Soon Nazi armies overran Europe, threatening to drive freedom from the face of the earth.

Then came D-day. Brave young men gave their lives on the stormy beaches of Normandy. They died so that we might live.

Finally the long war was over. Unbounded joy swept through the land. Peace returned. Freedom was preserved for our children.

Imagine—if the end of World War II brought such joy to the world, how will we feel when Jesus comes again? Picture that day, if you can. The Son of God moving toward earth through star-spangled space, attended by millions of angels. And then He calls out with a voice of thunder, "Awake, ye that sleep in the dust of the earth. Arise to everlasting life."

That voice calling our beloved dead will be heard the world around. Families will be reunited. Children snatched away by death will be placed again in their parents' arms. What a glad reunion day!

What does this mean to you? What does it mean to me? It means that there is something better beyond this day!

Think for a moment. Think what that day will mean to the crippled, to the blind, to those weakened by disease, as well as to minds confused by fear.

But think what it will mean to the able-bodied and the strong, to those who love life and want to live. You see, death may even seem welcome to a body racked by disease and pain. But to the strong and youthful, death can mean only disappointed hopes, disillusionment, shattered ambitions.

Here is the answer to death's sting. Not in anything man can do, but in the promise of the resurrection made by One who Himself demonstrated its possibility. Here is our hope!

Do you want to be ready for that day? You can be. All it takes is a heart surrendered to the Lord Jesus Christ. A mind willing to trust Him and follow Him wherever He leads.

Oh, friend, we can meet the Lord in peace when He returns to take us home. And He will be coming very soon. I urge you to make your reservation now.

For further information about the churches featured in this volume, please contact the following:

For the Lutherans:
 Lutheran Church—Missouri Synod
 1333 So. Kirkwood Road
 St. Louis, MO 63122
 (314) 965-9000

For the Baptists:
 Southern Baptist Convention
 901 Commerce Street, Suite 750
 Nashville, TN 37203
 (615) 244-2355

For the Methodists:
  InfoServ
  United Methodist Church
  P.O. Box 320
  Nashville, TN 37202
  (1-800) 251-8140

For the Charismatics:
  Demos Shakarian
  Full Gospel Businessmen's Fellowship International
  P.O. Box 5050
  Costa Mesa, CA 92626
  (714) 754-1400

For the Catholics:
  Archdiocese
  Pastoral Center
  501 Eastern Avenue
  P.O. Box 29260
  Washington, DC 20017

For our Jewish Friends:
  Please contact your nearest synagogue.

For the Adventists
  Adventist Information Services
  (1-800) 253-3000 (USA)
  (1-800) 327-1300 (Canada)
  or write:
  It Is Written
  P.O. Box 0
  Thousand Oaks, CA 91360

- LUTHER RESCUED JUSTIFICATION BY FAITH, THE ANABAPTISTS BROUGHT US THE PRINCIPLES of RELIGIOUS LIBERTY and BAPTISM BY IMMERSION, METHODISTS SHOWED HOW CONVERSION, FOLLOWED BY SANCTIFICATION OR GROWTH, DEVELOPS THE CHRISTIAN.   PAGE 36

- CHARISMATICS — TONGUES   PAGE 49
- SEE BLUE DOT, PG 52 ~ TONGUES
- HEALING... PG 53

- 1562 JAN. 18, CATHOLIC CHURCH CHANGED SABBATH INTO SUNDAY PG 67 and PG. 68
- NOW, NO LONGER DOES CHURCH HONER 10 COMMANDMENTS BUT 8.